Work: The Shadow and the Substance

David Bleakley

WORK: THE SHADOW AND THE SUBSTANCE

A reappraisal of life and labour

SCM PRESS LTD

334 01812 9

First published 1983
by SCM Press Ltd
26–30 Tottenham Road London N1

Phototypeset by Input Typesetting Ltd
and printed in Great Britain by
Richard Clay Ltd (The Chaucer Press)
Bungay, Suffolk

CONTENTS

To
Lewis Mumford – Master Pathfinder

PROLOGUE

We are between a death and a difficult birth (*Samuel Beckett*).

Recently I went on a tour of the shipyard where I worked during the early post-war years. In those days some 30,000 were employed; now the place, reduced to 6,000, seemed deserted. And as my guide put it, 'You've seen nothing yet. Come back in ten years and there will hardly be a man about the place.'

Little wonder that men and women feel disturbed about the 'new industrial revolution' in which they are invited to participate.

In 1981, *In Place of Work* was written as a 'tract for the times', presenting the point of view of those who feel threatened by new technology. It argued that we must begin to lose our illusions about the industrial background from which we have come; that we should prepare for a new industrial order; and that through a 'Sufficient Society' we could find liberation and salvation. That argument stands, but meantime the debate has widened.

Work: The Shadow and the Substance is more a handbook about adaptation and survival – about how the struggle is going and about the strategies which are emerging. It tells of encounters with industrial groups throughout the country and of the hopes and fears of those on the receiving end of industrial change. It records the fundamental reappraisal that is taking place as men and women in all walks of life begin to face up to the social and economic realities which confront them. Above all, *Shadow and Substance* is a plea that these people be heard in any debate about the shape of industrial development that takes place. Stress will be laid on their views in the chapters which follow.

It is also of particular importance to build bridges between those who analyse and those who demand urgent action. It is, for instance, not enough to argue (as I have heard it argued in many distinguished quarters) that people 'must learn to adjust', when what is really meant is that *someone else* must make the adjustment.

I recall E. F. Schumacher's remark: 'We all know that the human being has a marvellous fortitude in tolerating the suffering of others.' In real life the knowledge that cost-of-living expenses have to be met greatly concentrates the mind. The words of a printing trade operative come home with force: 'When are our armchair philosophers going to learn that we need real work and need it now?'

The 'now factor' is vital in programmes for practical living. I heard the factor in the distress of a worried employer with a long-established small family business, haunted by the fear that 'on one of these Friday nights I may not be able to raise the £5000 I need to pay my workers'. And the 'now factor' was painfully there in the plea of the unemployed youngster at the Drop-In Centre: 'I've done nothing since I left school three years ago. What do I do if I *never* get a job; lying in bed at night I come out in a cold sweat when I think of that.'

Fears like these are genuine and worthy of our concern; society needs to share the 'cold sweat' of that youngster.

But parallel with these understandable fears there is a growing recognition that a process of social and industrial change has started from which, in its broad outline, there can be no turning back. It is clear, for instance, that there is less tendency than in the past to blame the machine; it is recognized that deeper forces are at work. Even the politicians are regarded increasingly as being trapped by circumstances over which they have little ultimate control and which require something more than a party political response.

This awareness of a new dimension to our problems is ill-defined, but it is there. In a 'collective unconsciousness', it shares something of the flavour of Langdon Gilkey's noted comment on our times, made in a paper given to the Institute for Ecumenical and Cultural Research in June 1981:

> It seems to many of us that in the latter half of the twentieth century, we find ourselves in the midst of cognative, cultural and socio-political changes of vast importance, possibly of the scope represented by the development of Enlightenment sensibilities in the seventeenth and eighteenth centuries. . . It is impossible even

> in the midst of the most important historical transformation to see clearly what is afoot. Only afterwards can historical commentators see that a new epoch has begun or an old one ended. Let us settle for the fact that it *feels* as if we were reaching the end of an historical era and that *reflection* on the elements making up that feeling tends to substantiate it.

Gilkey's feeling is widely sensed, particularly among those who are involved in the industrial relations scene. I have met it in trade union meetings, in business groups and, increasingly these days, in national and international church gatherings. Prominent, too, among the 'new era' people are Manpower Services Commission officials whose on-the-spot grant decisions can do much to make or mar local community enterprise.

What is coming through from a widening constituency of concern is growing agreement that some accommodation must be made with new technology – *always providing* that a national bargain can be struck which will ensure that 'adjustment costs' are fairly divided across the nation. It is unrealistic and unjust to expect a significant proportion of our citizens to accept permanent downgrading in a society which, for all its problems, is in possession of great wealth.

The bargain to be struck will be to do with fundamentals – about the sharing of the gifts of technology, about relationships between wages and work, about the balance between traditional labour and choice activities, about definitions of work. We are also in need of an appropriate vocabulary to give meaning to the new concepts which must emerge. Such questions, often ignored by vested interests in political and economic pressure groups, are being confronted by men and women all over the country as they prepare to take part in what will be a new social order.

It is also the argument of *Shadow and Substance* that our country *can* survive the great transition. We face desperate problems, but, equally, our potential in experience, skill and material resources is great. And basically we have really little alternative but to try; we have nowhere else to go. More constructively, and as Kenneth Boulding once reminded us, it does no harm occasionally to say to ourselves: 'This happens to be my planet. I am very much attached to it, and I am desperately anxious that this particular experiment should be a success.' Wise words, indeed.

The call to hope is underpinned by the superb assurance of fellow

American prophet, Martin Luther King, that, whatever the problems of social change, no midnight long remains; and that there is a faith which 'adjourns the assemblies of hopelessness and brings new light into the dark chambers of pessimism'.

Something of that faith is needed as we move into a new industrial order. This book is about the men and women – Pathfinders, as one chapter describes them – who will make that order possible.

1

THE WITHERING OF WORK

> I never thought I'd see it, but it's the 1930s all over again (Liverpool docker).

In 1933 Ernest Bevin, General Secretary of the Transport and General Workers' Union, wrote his famous pamphlet, *My Plan for 2,000,000 Workless*. It was a passionate call by the 'Dockers' KC' for national action, so that 'the tortures suffered by the victims of the present system – who may never again secure employment – will be removed for ever.

In today's conditions the call of fifty years ago has a 1980s ring about it. Bevin had taken note of the Chancellor of the Exchequer's view that notwithstanding all that parliament might do to restore the trade of the country, new technical developments would continue to reduce the need for labour; he now asked for justice for those disturbed or displaced by the measures taken in the reorganization and development of industry.

> No longer should it be left to haphazard chance. The adjustment of hours and the acceptance of obligations to meet the revolutionary upset in the lives of the working people which these changes involve should be placed on an organized basis.

Ever the realist, there was a frank admittance that technological advance would reduce the need for labour:

> Thousands of the people displaced by machinery are the best workmen and craftsmen in the old processes and because their techniques and skills are not required by the new processes they have no chance today of being absorbed into industry when trade increases as the result of improved methods of production.

And, as today, there was special concern about the plight of young people:

> I plead for the young people and ask that a resolute national effort be made in order that they may be given the chance to which they are entitled.

There was also a call to the church:

> I would appeal to the religious bodies to come together and reach agreement on this problem. Surely they must see that no amount of dogma and no amount of preaching can undo the mischief and terrible moral harm done to children as the result of running the streets after leaving school.

Far ahead of his time, Ernest Bevin saw the need to approach the problem on the basis that unemployment must be accepted as a national liability. He proposed a complete survey of the working population for which industry or the state must find employment or a satisfactory system of maintenance:

> If this survey were taken of the insurable population it would be discovered, taking a ten years' view and having regard to the inevitable changes that must take place, that it would be extremely difficult to find employment for all the available people, even with limiting the employable period of life to the years between eighteen and sixty.

Then in a statement of principle appropriate to our own day Bevin welcomed higher productivity policies, provided they were combined with fair shares. He did not complain of less toil; he welcomed it:

> But I do complain of a system under which when industries are reorganized, one section of the community is made prosperous, whilst another section is left to starve. If we are to have the economic state, let us begin in the right way.'[1]

The intervention of World War II seemed to close the debate as the military machine created demands which led to industrial revival and a great expansion in the labour force. Once again we had been 'saved' by our greatest wastrel – more recently we have witnessed something of the same effect as, for a short time, work was boosted in arms establishments throughout the land by the Falklands crisis.

For many saved from unemployment, guns and butter seemed to go together.

Sadly, much of the problem of modern economics is still about turning spears into pruning hooks. Is it any wonder that many in our land today get the feeling that they have been here before?

William Keegan, *The Observer* economic correspondent, can be excused his cynical comment:

> If, as in 1939, the Polish crisis were to precipitate a war-time economy in Europe, the unemployment problem would recede rapidly. Out would go such arcane shibboleths as the public sector borrowing requirement; in would come the war effort, production targets and so on.[2]

Even the debate among parliamentarians has changed little: unemployment is the fault of the other side.

Mrs Thatcher: (9.10.82): 'Today's unemployed are the victims of yesterday's mistakes. Government destroyed jobs by fuelling inflation, trade unions destroyed jobs by restrictive practices, militants destroyed jobs by driving customers away.'

Mr Foot: (3.11.82): 'The Rt Hon. Lady must at last accept her responsibilities. She is responsible for what is happening. When will she face the havoc that her policies have created for industry?'

Mr Jenkins: (12.10.82): 'Sir Geoffrey Howe has one deficiency which is unfortunate in the holder of his particular office. He has practically no understanding of how the British economy really works. The government's economic policy is a route to penury and a road to despair. The direction must be changed, but not to the Labour Party's path. At best, any future Labour government would be a disorganized hypocrisy, saying one thing and doing another, and at worst a single ticket to Eastern Europe.'

The confrontation in politics has its counterpart in industrial relations. At its 1982 Congress the TUC rejected a pro-incomes policy statement and went on to endorse a resolution supporting free collective bargaining and rejecting 'discussions on pay restraint with this or any other government' – a wages stance described in a *Guardian* Leader as 'a vote for chaos'.

A few weeks later management entered the fray, with a similar stance. Summing up on the CBI annual conference, *The Times* reported:

> The CBI Conference threw out all thoughts of an incomes policy and the idea of a national economic forum to provide a background of information for the determination of pay levels. Instead, it carried a motion believing that competition is a better basis for national prosperity than incomes policy.[3]

But if there is evidence of the continuation of a crude political/industrial contest there are also indications that the traditional power game is being questioned increasingly by public opinion. Signals are being given that the survival instinct is beginning to assert itself as more and more the nation begins to discern the outlines of what begins to look like a new social order. Currently the pressures are being expressed in terms of commercial and industrial change but, deep down, whole communities begin to sense that something fundamental is happening to them.

E. F. Schumacher's judgment begins to ring true: 'This is not a recession. This is the end of an era.'[4]

The retreat from conventional politics is signalled by apathy at by-elections. For example, in November 1982, at a time when, reportedly, the economic 'blackspots' were 'seething with anger and bitterness', most of the London voters of Peckham and half of the voters of Midlands Northfield simply stayed at home.

However the political blamelayers may argue, there is a growing national (and international) consensus that no one political group can or will do anything fundamental about the present job crisis.

Equally perceptive is a *Guardian* Leader comment:

> A pall of fatalism has descended on the land. As in the thirties when revolution was forecast, apathy reigns. When Ministers say it is all the fault of the rest of the world, their predecessors or a hundred other circumstances entirely beyond their control, people now begin to believe them.[5]

This assessment found confirmation in the National Opinion Poll published by *The Observer* (5.9.82). More than two-thirds of the sample thought that none of the political parties had the right answer to cure unemployment and as many as 64% said that they did not believe politicians who said they could solve unemployment. Indeed, nowadays a politician is as likely to be howled down for promising immediate relief as for suggesting that the figure is likely to rise. For many, the hall-mark of success is being able to point to a slowing up in the *rate* of increase!

On such a view (which poses a challenge to those who value our democratic institutions) there is justification for the growing conviction that people are responding less to what the 'leaders' of our public opinion tell them than to the facts of life which confront them.

What, then, are the features of the new industrial landscape which is emerging in our country? How is it going to affect our working lives – and how, in particular, is unemployment affecting the most vulnerable sections of the nation?

The size of the problem

In January 1983 the unemployment figure reached 3,096,997 – a dramatic figure for a country that has enjoyed virtually full employment for several decades. Forecasts by government agencies suggest that the three million mark will be normal for the foreseeable future; less favourable indicators point to a rise to five million or more. Additional difficulties may emerge as a result of technological acceleration. For example, in a recent *Credo* programme TV researcher Barrie Sherman estimated that four to five million jobs would be at risk because of new technology in the next decade.

But beyond the numbers problem there are changes in the pattern of unemployment which are new and disturbing. Long-term unemployment is growing. The Manpower Services Commission forecast in 1982 that over 40% of Britain's 3.3 million jobless would experience at least twelve months redundancy and by 1984 over half the country's unemployed would suffer the experience of a year or more on the dole, a situation likely to persist for the rest of the eighties.

Ever longer-term periods are envisaged for large numbers. It is already clear that the number of people jobless for more than two years has risen sharply and even if unemployment stabilizes at around three million it is expected that the long-term unemployed will remain at around 1.2 million.

Chronic unemployment is particularly insidious in a society which makes little real provision for those without jobs. Two months out of work is an inconvenience; two years may be a disaster. Certainly for many today the fear of 'never working again in my life' has become a growing reality.

Youth unemployment

Ticking away in the statistics is the 'time bomb' of youth unemployment. Many adults can cope with unemployment because of supportive experience and the possession of social skills on which they can draw. And, of course, older workers see work 'warts and all' and are often appreciative of leisure opportunities especially if their domestic commitments are being met. As one well-balanced man put it to me – 'For many of us it's not the job we miss, it's the security and extra-mural opportunities that the job makes possible.'

But the school-leavers have no such compensations; nor are they prepared for the shock of 'having nothing to do' when formal education is terminated. So emerges a threatened and frustrated generation (more than a million) who are increasingly alienated from a society which has failed them. Many of the nation's young people – our seed corn – have been unemployed for more than two years and in some areas over 70% are without jobs. Socially it could become our most divisive problem. American social scientist Martin Mayer makes the disturbing observation:

> By all indications, the generation now reaching maturity will be the first in history to be denied, as a group, nature's blessing of a death that relates to the end of the possibilities of a meaningful life.[6]

Many of these young people, particularly in the poorest areas of the country, have given up hope of ever being able to find work. And the desperation is evident in the comments they make. From a few collected from all over the country:

'I am eighteen and I've never worked in my life. My dad's out of work and the rest of the family. There just isn't any work around here. I wonder at times what I'll be like in three or four years' time. Just imagine, in your twenties, without ever working. Who'd give you a job with a record like that?'

'I suppose the Manpower people are doing their best with their training and all that. But its Junk Jobs we're asked to do. Something to keep us busy, not real work. I've a string of 'O' Levels but they're no use to me.'

'I've written hundreds of letters, but deep down I know it's no use. There's plenty more as good as me around and there's just no work. I read and watch television a lot and try to keep myself fit – but all I really need is a job. Any kind.'

The fear is there before school days end. A Birmingham teacher in a large comprehensive school says this about his final year pupils who are hit hard by the knowledge that jobs for 16-year olds have all but disappeared: 'They are very depressed. We have one girl who is positively suicidal; while the boys turn around and say that if they can't get what they want when they leave school they will go out and take it.'

These young people are typical of a dangerously high proportion of our young people for whom the promise of a transition from school to work is not taking place. They have a sense of a social contract being broken.

Peter Townsend gets to the heart of the matter in his comment on the effect of unemployment on young people brought up in a society governed by the worth ethic:

> People want to work because they are taught from childhood to fulfil themselves and earn their keep, and contribute to the community's needs; and the work they do is often necessary justification for their families and for themselves for their lives. That is why unemployment is such an appalling and undeserved indignity.[7]

Age and youth

And this crisis confronts the young at the very moment in history when a fundamental change is taking place in the numerical and social significance of those at the other end of the age scale – the over-60s.

This latter group, described at the 1982 United Nations World Assembly on Ageing as 'a valuable national resource', has become the fastest growing sector of the population. In fact, two-thirds of all people who ever lived to their sixtieth birthday are alive today; so, for the first time in human history men and women are surviving in sufficient numbers around the world to make up a new generation. According to the United Nations, by the year 2025 one person in seven will be over sixty compared with just one in every twelve in 1950. The impact of this emergent group will be substantial.

It is unlikely that this new generation, once it discovers its power as a pressure group in society, will be willing to continue to accept an inferior political and economic role in society especially as it becomes increasingly what has been called the 'healthy, wealthy and wise' group. In particular, while many of the over-60s will welcome well-pensioned retirement, others, denied that opportunity, will resist compulsory 'poverty' retirement (see below, Chapter 8).

There is throughout the world a growing campaign against 'ageism', and in the USA it is already illegal to job discriminate on the grounds of age. Pensioners constitute a considerable political lobby – if they are not 'heard', the day is approaching when we will witness the election of candidates on a specifically pensioners' 'ticket'.

Maggie Kuhn, founder of the 60,000 strong Grey Panthers network of young and old Americans campaigning, not just against 'ageism' but for all kinds of social reform, puts it bluntly:

> Ageism is the stereotyping and discrimination of people on the basis of age. The old are condemned to obsolescence; left to rot like wrinkled babies in glorified playpens – forced to succumb to a trivial, purposeless waste of their years and their time.[8]

It would be a tragedy if a scramble for jobs took place between two valuable groups – those who have a lifetime to give and those who have been giving for a lifetime. Better by far that the Young Lions and the Grey Panthers, who have so much in common and between whose generations there is so much natural rapport, should unite to seek justice for all.

But justice for all will involve more than one nation. As Willie Brandt and other globe watchers have warned, an international response is required to deal with a malfunctioning of the world economy which is making its effect felt in every region.

The interdependence of the world is underlined in overseas unemployment statistics. As the jobless in Britain passed the three million mark the EEC reported a record eleven million jobless of which 40% were under 25 years. In the same month the normally stable German economy reached nearly two million unemployed, with the government describing the figure as 'an alarming signal that should worry everyone'.

Encouragingly, the nations of Western Europe have responded to the threat by passing in a special session of the Assembly of the Council of Europe a series of remarkable resolutions 'on the fight against unemployment' – remarkable both in their unanimity and in the range of remedies offered.

Recommendation 948 (1982), as the decision is described, is one of the most important consensus documents to have been produced by Western Europe since World War II. Its stress on the need for joint action is particularly important as is its declaration that 'strategies based only on growth and the market's traditional powers of recovery can no longer be realistically viewed as effective against unemployment and its effects, but that the appropriate context is an active social policy pursued by member states in concert'.

The document offers an enlightened analysis and a programme of action to all who believe in a wider-than-the-nation-state response to the social and economic problems of our time:

PARLIAMENTARY ASSEMBLY
OF THE COUNCIL OF EUROPE

Thirty-fourth Ordinary Session

RECOMMENDATION 948 (1982)[1]
on the fight against unemployment

The Assembly,

1. Noting that unemployment currently affects appoximately 17 million people in the Council of Europe member countries, and that, according to the current economic outlook, this figure is expected to continue to rise throughout at least the next year;

2. Further noting that, quite apart from the numbers affected, certain qualitative symptoms are more acute now than at any stage since the war, including youth unemployment, unemployment among women, the lengthening of the average duration of unemployment, the proliferation of illicit work, regional imbalances and the worsening plight of migrant workers who in some cases face an upsurge of xenophobia;

3. Considering that, if this situation continues, it could have

1. *Assembly debate* on 30 September 1982 (11th Sitting) (see Doc. 4953, report of the Committee on Social and Health Questions).
Text adopted by the Assembly on 30 September 1982 (11th Sitting).

extremely serious social and political consequences and pose a threat to democratic institutions;

4. Noting that some of the causes of the deterioration in the employment situation are structural, such as population trends, technological change and fiercer international competition, with the attendant risk of a return to protectionism;

5. Pointing out, however, that policies which underestimate the State's responsibility for achieving and maintaining full employment and rely solely on a self-regulating free market have proved more and more incapable of bringing the situation under control;

6. Considering that strategies based only on growth and the market's traditional powers of recovery can no longer be realistically viewed as effective against unemployment and its effects, but that the appropriate context is an active social policy pursued by member states in concert;

7. Regretting that the right to work, which is widely acknowledged as a fundamental social right and is no more than a safeguard enabling every individual to earn his own livelihood, is still far from having constitutional force in all member states;

8. None the less recalling the fundamental principles laid down in Article 1 of the European Social Charter, which contains an undertaking to create conditions for the effective exercise of the right to work, *inter alia* by achieving and maintaining a high and stable level of employment;

9. Being convinced that the success of measures against unemployment will depend largely on the achievement of a social consensus which requires sincere solidarity on the part of everyone in employment, in particular in the framework of negotiations between management and labour which should be conducted in a spirit of collective responsibility towards their 'third partner', those who are unemployed;

10. Considering that some fifteen million foreigners – migrant workers and their familys – are living in Council of Europe member countries, and that their number is growing every year as a result of family reunion and births;

11. Considering that migrant workers have contributed substantially to the economic expansion of the immigration countries during

the past twenty years, and that the economy of many European countries will still need their help in the future;

12. Recognising that central government's responsibility for combating unemployment, and the measures this necessarily entails, can usefully be supplemented from the potential available to regional and local authorities;

13. Considering it logical that, instead of paying a high price for the consequences of unemployment:

(a) new jobs should be created by State and State-sponsored investment and this investment should be economically rational;

(b) viable private investment should be encouraged by public aid, which should be linked to the creation of new jobs;

(c) this aid could be funded by taxes and levies imposed over a limited period of time, the principle of solidarity that those in remunerated employment should contribute towards surmounting the unemployment of others, and that this contribution should respect the principles of social justice;

14. Recognising that a reorganisation of working time could make a major contribution to reducing unemployment;

15. Being convinced that, among the various possible strategies, whether geared to increasing the volume of work available or to redistributing it, priority must go to those whose implementation does not involve long delays;

16. Recommends that the Committee of Ministers call on the governments of member states:

i. to make it their policy to aid investment in schemes which are likely to result in protection of existing jobs or creation of new jobs;

ii. to pay special attention to labour-market policies, fiscal incentives and other selective measures with a view to increasing significantly investment and employment in both the public and private sectors;

iii. to promote decentralisation of opportunities to work and greater worker mobility by setting up, in association with local authorities, programmes of relocation aid, possibly with provision for removal and rehousing grants;

iv. to develop, as key features of occupational life, programmes of initial and further vocational training, *inter alia*:

- by instituting a compulsory year of basic vocational training at the end of normal schooling, designed, in particular, to meet the needs of the new technologies and with the object of reducing the number of young people without vocational qualifications;
- by developing means to assist the transition from theoretical instruction to the reality of working life, for example the alternation of instruction with work experience (training *en alternance*), which both young people and older workers with adjustment problems require;
- by requiring enterprises either to develop their training arrangements or pay a payroll and turnover tax to help finance the provision of training;

v. to take vigorous action against illicit work, impose strict limits on overtime and introduce regulations on temporary work – which has increased alarmingly – in order to safeguard fully workers' economic and social rights;

vi. to enforce the prohibition of children's employment;

vii. to consider the following measures to reorganise time at work:

(a) a general reduction in the working year through measures to introduce greater flexibility and give the individual greater freedom of choice by:

- a gradual shortening of the working week and working day by means of collective sectoral negotiation;
- longer annual holidays and general provision for extended (sabbatical) leave;
- more opportunities for part-time work, together with adequate social protection;
- the introduction of a fifth team for continuous shift work;

(b) measures to shorten working life, such as adjustments in pension schemes to enable individuals to decide their age of retirement, financial inducements to retire early, pre-retirement arrangements offering shorter hours in the final years of working life in order to ease the transition to retirement;

viii. *(a)* to take into account the measures recommended in Committee of Ministers Resolution (78) 4, on the social and economic impact on migrant workers of economic recession or crisis, bearing especially in mind the principle that migrant workers and their families should not be used as a pool of reserve labour, deprived of security of employment, for correcting market fluctuations;

(b) to grant second generation migrants a legal status recognising the right to remain and to work in the receiving country;

(c) to ratify the European Convention on the Legal Status of Migrant Workers, which has not yet entered into force since it has been ratified by only four states: Portugal, Spain, Sweden and Turkey;

(d) to continue to give priority to questions relating to migrants in the Council of Europe medium-term plan and the Intergovernmental Work Programme;

ix. to have regard, in all bilateral and multilateral trade agreements, to fundamental social rights and international labour regulations in the 'cheap labour countries', with a view to approximating their social welfare standards to those of Europe, and to ensure that free competition is not distorted by inequalities in labour costs;

17. Calls on the Committee of Ministers to forward this recommendation to the governments of member states without delay, with a particular view to its discussion at the 2nd Conference of European Ministers for Labour, to be held in 1983;

18. Recommends that the Committee of Ministers implement within the Council of Europe the principles set out in this recommendation, particularly as regards the flexible lowering of the retirement age and regulations governing temporary work.

These recommendations, and particularly 9, 17 and 18, are likely to have a considerable influence on the policies of governments linked to the Council of Europe. The practical suggestions for implementation are of special importance for policy makers in the member states and will have considerable influence on the shape of the agenda for future international economic conferences. The Recommendation 948 is a historic call which may enable Europe to become a trail blazer for other threatened continents.

It is certainly clear that the malfunctioning of economies is not solely a 'European disease'. In Australia miners and steel workers have been marching on Parliament House in Canberra with a chant of 'We want jobs', while in far-away, rich Canada, the Immigration

Minister has cited the employment situation as his reason for reducing sharply the intake of immigrants. In the United States, too, the concern is great.

Equally, Japan, which has done so much to boost robotics exports, is beginning to feel the effects at home of the application of advanced technology. Recent reports indicate that under-employment is becoming endemic and, as in Western Europe, the Japanese begin to fear that automation may not generate enough new jobs to replace those which are being lost to their 'wonder machines'. And (ironic-sounding to British shipbuilders) the Japanese are also feeling the pinch of competition from South Korea and complain of loss of orders to that increasingly competitive industrial new nation.

Even China does not seem to be sufficiently 'closed' to escape the problem. Figures released by the Shanghai Labour Bureau report that as many as 10% of workers in state-owned industry are surplus to production requirements. 'Unemployment' as such is not admitted by Chinese commentators, but the official description of 'waiting for jobs' may be in many respects a euphemism for old fashioned 'unemployment', as the People's Republic finds increasing difficulty in coping with its seven million annual school leavers and its yearly population increase of over ten million.

And, as always, the developing countries suffer disproportionately. Giles Merritt reminds us in his complacency shattering study *World Out of Work*[9] that jobless forecasts for industrial nations are insignificant compared to those of the Third World. It is estimated that there are about 300–500 million unemployed in the developing nations and that by the turn of the century the demographic figures suggest 900 million or possibly one billion people without jobs.

The scale of this emergency requires a qualitative change in our approach to international economics. We are being challenged to reorder our economic relationship in ways which bring justice into the world-wide market place.

Here the church is expected to give, and is well placed to give, a lead. A recent appeal in the *International Review of Mission* underlined the challenge:

> How could it be otherwise now that the Christian churches have at last realized that the defence and promotion of human rights is an integral part of their mission? Any religion that claims to champion human rights cannot remain deaf to the cries of the

> poor in the contemporary world, rent by the widening gulf between the rich nations and the poor nations. Out of a population of about 4,000 million it is estimated that at least 800 million suffer from malnutrition.[10]

In a world where the future of Christianity is more and more being decided in continents other than Europe it is important for 'rich world' churches to grasp this fact and to acknowledge that in today's situation evangalization of the poor is seen increasingly as a criterion of the authenticity of the churches' mission.

Some measure of how far the richer nations 'walk by on the other side' emerges in the weakness of the response by national governments to the Brandt North-South Report, and the even more disappointing outcome of the 1981 Cancun Conference on world poverty. The rebuke is all the more justified when we reflect on what is possibly the gravest of today's human statistics published by the United Nations: we are told that world population may reach 10.5 thousand million by 2110 AD. Some estimates go as high as fifteen thousand million. On the shorter run it is generally agreed that only a disaster of appalling magnitude could now prevent the population from reaching six thousand million by the end of the present century.

Clearly we are being called to be one another's keeper on a massive scale. But it is a challenge that must not deter us. At last we are moving into the truly divine economic dimension – we are beginning to discover that we are one human family as we react together to the malfunctioning of a global economy on which we are increasingly interdependent. Confronted by the economic facts of life we may begin to grasp the meaning of life itself.

Uniquely among human institutions the church is well-placed to act for humanity, challenging the international conscience and inspiring vast numbers of men and women to a sacrificial response. At personal and national levels John V. Taylor's *Enough is Enough* continues to rebuke and warn us; and on a global scale we are in need of something like William James' 'moral equivalent to war'. Clearly it will not be easy. But equally clearly we face a new age of mission in which Christians, if their faith is to have any credibility, must respond creatively.

2

A NEW COVENANT WITH THE MACHINE

> 'I suppose if Joe Wade says there's no alternative we will have to go along. But I don't like it – machines always destroy more jobs than they create' (London printer facing the new technology).

The uneasy relationship between wage-earners and the machine is well brought out in *The Ragged Trousered Philanthropists*, Robert Tressall's classic novel of working-class life written during the great slump of the 1930s. Some of Tressall's characters in a meal-hour discussion have decided that 'the exterminating machine' may be the cause of economic misery.

> 'I don't see no sense in always grumbling', said Crass. 'These things cannot be altered; you cannot expect there can be plenty of work for everyone with all this labour-saving machinery what's been invented.'
>
> 'Of course', said Harlow, 'the people what used to be employed on the work what's now done by machinery has to find something else to do. Some of them goes to our trade, for instance. The result is there's too many at it, and there ain't enough work to keep them all going.' 'Yes' cried Crass eagerly, 'that's just what I say. Machinery is the real cause of all the poverty.'

Frank Owen, Tressall's favourite philosopher, intervened:

> 'Machinery is undoubtedly the cause of unemployment,' replied Owen, 'but it's not the cause of poverty; that's another matter altogether.'
>
> 'Well, it seems to me to amount to the same thing,' said Harlow and nearly everyone agreed.

Owen explained:

> 'It doesn't seem to me to amount to the same thing. In my opinion we are all in a state of poverty even when we have employment. The condition we are reduced to when we are out of work is more properly described as destitution.'

Owen continued:

> 'Poverty consists in a shortage of the necessities of life. When those things are so scarce and so dear that people are unable to obtain sufficient of them to satisfy all their needs, they are in a condition of poverty. If you think that the machinery which makes it possible to produce all the necessaries of life in abundance is the cause of the shortage, it seems to me that there must be something wrong with your minds.'[1]

Such opposition on the part of those who felt threatened by machinery was natural and in the absence of reasonable guarantees must always be expected (it is remarkable that the intelligent innovators who pioneeer new technology do not recognize this fact of life and make provision for it).

In particular, given the memories of the first industrial revolution the machine has symbolized for most workers a threat to life and limb and livelihood. Even today the legacy lingers on. A recent survey indicated that 65% of the jobless blamed higher technology for their plight and there is a good deal of evidence that 'higher productivity' has had to bribe its way into the workshop.[2] To those so threatened Luddism has always seemed an obvious response, with each generation's Ned Ludd being accorded the status of a respected industrial freedom fighter who knows his people's problems.

Equally persistent has been the support from champions of the machine. Factory masters in general have been critical of those who have opposed the introduction of machinery and have argued that the long-term benefits would more than make up for any temporary inconvenience to the work force. In this they had the support of Adam Smith who condemned trade union activity as 'a conspiracy against the public'. Smith, and the distinguished economists who followed his lead, certainly recognized the likelihood of periodic slumps and considerable disruption in the lives of those displaced by machinery but they had little to say that was of help to the victims. This disregard of a great social problem was only possible due to the powerlessness of the operatives of the time. Nowadays there has been a dramtic change in the industrial balance of power in favour of the working class. The balance is such that a repeat of the injustices of the first industrial revolution would certainly be resisted.

Yet the arguments down the centuries have not changed all that much. Typical of the political establishment of Smith's time was a House of Lords Debate in 1812 on machine-breaking. The official view was given by the Earl of Lauderdale who condemned Luddism, not only because of its revolutionary implications, but because he believed that the workers would ultimately stand to benefit from improvements in productivity.

> Nothing could be more certain than the fact that every improvement in machinery contributes to the improvement in the condition of persons manufacturing the machines, there being in a very short time after such improvements were introduced a greater demand for labour than ever before.[3]

(I wonder what the Noble Earl would think about the December 1982 Luddite plan by the government to compensate steel owners willing to break up steel making plants so as to ensure their withdrawal from the productive process.) So began a debate which has continued into our own day – and now assumes fresh urgency as a new generation and new species of machine makes its appearance.

Influential voices on both sides of industry still accept the optimistic scenario – nowadays increasingly bolstered up by the intellectual persuasiveness of Milton Friedmann's 'Free to Choose' philosophy. Those who trust in the power of self-regulatory mechanisms to see us through point with confidence to the great expansion of employment which has accompanied previous developments in technology. History, it is argued, will repeat itself. In particular, we are advised that modern society can expect a 'spin-off' in new employment which will make up for any job displacement caused by electronic technology. The fact that the figures do not yet add up is explained as a matter of 'delayed delivery dates'; patience is the counsel given. And when it is protested that sufficient jobs of the right kind may not appear in the right place at the right time – at that point something like the 'invisible hand' is brought in as the long-run guarantor for economic stability.

Even the most modern captains of industry, faced with job decline on a massive scale, are prone to regard the current crisis as a shaking-out process which will lead to better times. A good example is car industrialist, Sir Michael Edwardes. In the eye of his own considerable storm, Sir Michael manages to strike a buoyant note. At the 1982 CBI Conference, in a British Leyland version of 'what is good for General Motors is good for America', delegates heard from this influential leader that he was not impressed by arguments which suggested that increased productivity would lead to longer dole queues. For Sir Michael the really significant facts were those which showed that between 1860 and 1960 productivity trebled and the size of the work force doubled. The German car industry was quoted as an example of what could be done – in that country the industry had greatly improved its productivity after 1945, which benefited employment, because it increased the nation's share of the world market. But the reverse was the case in Britain where, in many cases, productivity was abysmal. And, Sir Michael concluded, that was why BL had cut its manning by 93,000 in order to redress the balance.[4]

This tunnel vision is shared by many in industry who, undoubtedly hard pressed, are having to look to their own particular 'patch'. For such as they, survival is naturally enough the name of the game. But the social consequences of labour-shedding on a vast scale by great industrial enterprises cannot be ignored – we are required to have a collective responsibility to the greater pattern which is the community. In this respect, broader and deeper considerations arise for the nation which cannot be dealt with on the basis of an 'ourselves alone' philosophy. Already there are alarming indications that the 'invisible hand' is unable to make provision for the massive numbers being displaced as major industries attend to their 'own affairs'. In industry, as in other areas of life, no man is an island.

It is all too obvious that there is a serious difference between the massive lay-off in labour in, say, steel (100,000) and the capacity for new technology developments to absorb such numbers. Even assuming that the workers concerned are adaptable, great problems to do with home transfers and the social impact on whole communities remain. In many areas the local industry *is* the community. To add to the difficulties of reabsorption there is growing concern that the office and service sector, long regarded as a sponge for surplus labour, will itself be subject to labour-saving pressures. An important survey carried out by the Association of Professional, Executive, Clerical and Computer Staff (APECCS) concludes:

> The implications of the micro-electronic revolution for the numbers in work, the nature of their work and the social organization of work and leisure, are enormous. The impact of new technology will be severe among those groups – young people, women and older workers – already more vulnerable to unemployment. The areas where micro-electronics will increase employment opportunities – computing, electronics engineering, skilled technicians – will not absorb unskilled young people. New capital investment in micro-electronics, computing and tele-communications will, in fact, have the overall effect of cutting labour requirements, since it is no longer the case that an increase in investment will automatically create new jobs.[5]

The report lists 29 occupations most likely to disappear or undergo radical change over the next decade.

There will, of course, be some compensating job creation and the development of advanced new skills. Kenneth Barnes, Director of Information Technology Year 1982, went so far in his introductory message as to claim that 'Britain's future depends on information technology and that knowing how to compute will be as important as being able to read and write. It is no exaggeration to say that the impact of IT will be greater than that of any other technical developments that have come before – the invention of steam power, the telephone or electricity all included. The implication for industry of all this can be summed up in a word – productivity. That productivity can lead to growth and hence to an expanding economy.' These are serious aims, but if they are to have real meaning they must be people-centred in their implementation. Technology's capacity to change the industrial landscape and with it much of our social framework is awesome. In such circumstances industry becomes too important to be left to the industrialists. A. D. Lindsay's plea for 'technology with the merciful heart' and a permeation of economics 'with the love of God and of our neighbour' is ever relevant. Without such a balance the future is bleak.

Getting from here to there

The new industrial order to which we are being pointed is no mere extension of the first industrial revolution; it stands on its own and has a societal transformation capacity unequalled by anything that has gone before. There are certainly signs today that we cannot take as our guide past industrial experience. With the development of solid state electronics, machines that have displaced human muscle in the productive process are themselves being replaced by machines that take over the functions of the brain. And, as we have seen, this is happening in the service industries also.

In sum: the relation between man and machine is undergoing a radical transformation; the easing of human toil by technology has entered a new and revolutionary stage bringing with it the challenge of momentous change in our social system. What William James once called 'the gospel of work' is up for radical revision.[6]

The call for such a revision is not new; it has been made by generations of Utopian writers who have speculated on the possibilities of a society without enforced labour. The machine has been seen as the vehicle which can carry us to a new future. In the present century a distinguished line of social philosophers have tried, largely without success, to concentrate our minds on the growing significance of the ubiquitous robot, with every decade providing a resurgence of literature on the subject. Even in the depth of the 1930s depression, a time when the topic seemed decidedly academic, the shape of 'states to come' when hard labour would be abolished was discussed. Most noted was a contribution from John Maynard Keynes who, writing about the future his grandchildren might face, had this to say:

> If the economic problem is solved mankind will be deprived of its traditional purpose. . . Thus for the first time since his creation man will be faced with his real, his permanent problem – how to use his freedom from pressing economic cares.
>
> There is no country and no people, I think, who can look forward to the problem for the ordinary person, with no special talents to occupy himself, especially if he no longer has roots in the soil or in custom or in the beloved conventions of a traditional society.

Keynes' conclusion was sombre:

> I think with dread of the readjustments of the habits and instincts of the ordinary man, bred into him for generations, which he may be asked to discard within a few decades. To those who sweat for their daily bread leisure is a longed-for sweet – until they get it.[7]

Bevin and Keynes, worlds apart in class and profession, were at one in their prophetic insight – the urgency of their forecast eased only temporarily by the intervention of war.

Nearer our own time the great German-American sociologist, Hannah Arendt, has alerted us to what she sees as a most threatening development:

> This is the advent of automation, which in a few decades probably will empty the factories and liberate mankind from its oldest and most natural burden, the burden of labouring and the bondage to necessity. Freedom from labour itself is not new; it once belonged among the most firmly established chores of the few. In this instance, it seems as though scientific progress and technical developments had been only taken advantage of to achieve something about which all former ages dreamed, but which none had been able to realize.

But Hannah Arendt discerns a more subtle and more dangerous challenge in the human condition:

> However, this is only in appearance. The modern age has carried with it a theoretical glorification of labour and has resulted in a factual transformation of the whole of society into a labouring class. It is a society of labourers which is about to be liberated from the fetters of labour and this society does no longer know of those higher and more meaningful activities for the sake of which this freedom would deserve to be won.

And a conclusion, like Keynes':

> What we are confronted with is the prospect of a society of labourers without labour, that is, without the only activity left to them. Surely nothing could be worse.[8]

Throughout the 1940s, from his great knowledge of the tension between new methods of production and conventional economics, Norbert Wiener made the same point with greater urgency, but with little marked success:

> Let us remember that the automatic machine, whatever we think of any feeling it may have or not have, is the precise economic equivalent of slave labour. Any labour which competes with slave labour must accept the economic conditions of slave labour. It is

> perfectly clear that this will produce an unemployment situation, in comparison with which the present recession and even the depression of the thirties will seem a pleasant joke.[9]

All three of these commentators conclude on a sombre note offering little consolation to those who have to deal with the 'nuts and bolts' of social engineering. Still less is there any evidence of a questioning of the morality of a social system which 'makes progress' at the expense of those at the bottom of the social pile least able to defend themselves.

What *is* abundantly clear is that we are ill-prepared nationally (and even more so internationally) for the massive reorganization of society and an 'economics of sharing' on which we are required to embark as a condition of survival. Our unpreparedness could hardly be otherwise in an age dominated by tear-away industrial expansion with its 'buy now – pay later' life-styles.

Sadly, the future has caught up with us; 'later' has become 'now'. It is a pity that our philosophers have not been heard. But in the world inhabited by Lord Keynes' 'ordinary man' the consolations of philosophy are few and far between. For such as these, talk of new social strategies is pretty high-powered stuff – more often than not they just want to know how to get around the next corner of life.

In these circumstances the problems of transition are more easily stated than solved. For millions at the 'sharp end' of the process of adaptation in this and other lands the key question, however seemingly mundane, remains – how *does* one retain a working pattern sufficient to provide for the everyday requirements of home and family while at the same time becoming part of a new social order? The question has been put to me at discussions in every region in the country and from every work and social situation. It is a profoundly human question – the stuff of real life. A truly national response is needed so that, united as a nation, we can search out the practical propositions which will enable our community institutions (and though they creak severely, at this stage they are not easily replaced or refurbished) to provide the planning and administrative back-up involved in the 'great transition'. However much we may hope for (and must work for) a restructuring of our national institutions, it is likely that they will be around for some time to come. What we need is an interim strategy that will get us on our way.

Much of this strategy is emerging as in every part of the land (and in many parts of the world) alternatives to the social and economic patterns which derive in large part from the first industrial revolution are being explored. In the field of job creation, for example, a triple alliance, unthinkable a few years ago, is beginning to emerge between government and both sides of industry. 'Sacred cows' are being quietly sacrificed. Private citizens are also actively forming groups to promote 'alternative activities' and there is now a considerable body of organizations providing supporting services for local enterprises of all kinds. The literature of alternatives flourishes and a network for Alternative Technology and Technology Assessment has been established at the Open University Centre in Milton Keynes. Over one hundred pages of *Small is Possible*, George McRobie's tribute to the late E. F. Schumacher, is devoted to listing information about alternative society groups at home and abroad. It is a formidable list, bearing evidence to the response, local and often spontaneous, which is taking place on a steadily growing scale. When effective 'linkage' takes place the separate experiments will constitute a formidable combination.

A hint of how to proceed during the interim period comes from that most down-to-earth researchers of social skills, Ralf Dahrendorf of the London School of Economics. Invited by the British Institute of Management to explore the employment problem, Dahrendorf was at first cautious about the future. He saw 'the cards stacked against change' and felt surrounded by official minds and vested interests deeply-rooted in the work society. Nor did he see much hope in the behaviour of some of our most vital institutions:

> Unions objecting to community services because of job displacement, universities unable to serve mature students because of the upset to traditional methods of time-tabling, and industrial relations participants who continue to play the costly adversary game.

Very much a picture of the real and frustrating world in which we live.

But Dahrendorf makes his most positive contribution when he makes plain his duty as a philosopher to *change* the world as well as to explain it:

> My only hope is that individuals, groups, even firms and organizations will find enough loopholes in society's creaking structures

to explore new ways and make the rigid organizations and ideas of yesterday obsolete. I for one shall do my best to contribute to this exercise in practical liberty.[10]

Liberty and the machine: what guarantees?

Dahrendorf's reference to practical liberty underlines the urgency of redefining the relationship between people and machines in ways which ensure that the sudden plenty made possible by the latest union of science and new technology will be used to release humanity from unnecessary labour and not to facilitate a new bondage.

The danger has long been noted by the anti-Utopians and perhaps most brilliantly popularized by Aldous Huxley's *Brave New World* and George Orwell's *Nineteen Eighty-Four*. More recently, Alvin Toffler has been carrying on a successful personal crusade to alert society to the dangers of uncontrolled technical innovation.

Toffler's concern has been powerfully reinforced by Massachusetts Institute of Technology top computer scientist Professor Weizenbaum, who in 1982 asked serious questions about the extent to which computers are being accorded the power to make judgments aided and abetted by the programmer who 'is the creator of universes for which he alone is the law giver'.

A leading science correspondent who recently interviewed Weizenbaum was told 'we are sleepwalking into a technology whose real influence, unless we wake up, will be far more malign than benign.' He concluded:

> I am coming to the conclusion that the computer is inherently anti-human – an invention of the devil.[11]

In Britain Giles Merritt in his popular guide *World Out of Work* makes the same point with equal force. In what he calls 'The Micro-Electronics Monster' we are warned:

> When trying to estimate the impact of electronics on work it is vital to emphasize that the micro-technology in question is still an unknown quantity. The temptation is to view it as an extension of the mechanical and electrical technology we are used to, when in fact it is more like a bio-genetic monster created by some mad scientist. It changes its nature and its substance before our very eyes and its ever growing tentacles reach out to grasp and

transfrom old industries and traditional work methods. A word processor may be the lineal descendant of a typewriter, but it is a distant cousin with a savage mutant strain.[12]

Such widely-held opinions are a powerful argument for control systems which will ensure that new technology is introduced in a form and at a pace compatible with the stability of society. Unfortunately it is in this respect that we are most in danger of failure. As I have argued elsewhere[13] we must ensure that there is parity of concern between efforts to promote new technology and the application of controls to ensure that such developments meet social and human needs. Here we must engage in a community response to technology which will involve government regulation, public participation in technology policy and the creation of alternative forms of industrial enterprise, technology and socio-economic organization more amenable to community control.

There is little evidence that public policies are reacting to this challenge and even the well-funded Information Technology Year proposals paid little attention to the social implications of their promotion. But we neglect the problem at our peril. The very least that we should do is to ensure that a sufficient proportion of our best scientists are sponsored by the government to study and advise on the short and long-term consequences of new technology and to promote appropriate control systems.

Certainly our present over-dependence on private citizens and dedicated pressure groups is no substitute for a national (and international) monitoring system adequately funded and staffed. The government, without giving much evidence of having grasped the full implications of what is happening, have pointed to the watershed nature of the changes with which new technology confronts us. A recent Department of Industry brochure had this to say:

> During a normal lifetime, most people don't have the chance to watch a revolution. For us, though, its different. Not only can we watch a revolution, we're all actively taking part in it.

In such circumstances it is not enough to leave things to chance or to assume that a self-correcting mechanism will work for the good of the community. What is needed is a control system which will ensure that technology is introduced in accordance with agreed principles that protect the society in which it is being given room to develop and which ultimately has to underwrite its cost.

Currently we are in danger of neglecting the development and application of such control systems or, worse still, we depend on the 'good sense' of vested interests representing capital and labour. Here if ever is a case for a church presence in the debate. To adapt William Temple: are we prepared to consider what are the fundamental facts which are directly relevant to the ordering of the new society which is quite evidently emerging; and can we ensure that Christian thought and action can be shaped to play a leading part in the re-ordering of society that must take place?

Enlightened self-interest, if nothing else, should convince us of the dangers of a two-nation situation arising with all its debiliting social consequences. Somehow we must encourage a great deal more intelligence in our social planning, combined with even more charity. That wisest of philosopher/engineers Dennis Gabor in an optimistic look to the future once reminded us in a passage about sharing one another's burdens:

> The leading minority must forget that the majority are 'objectively' useless because they could be replaced by machines. They must find their reward in the happiness of the common man, in a paternal feeling which must never show itself in paternalism.[14]

Gabor's minority and majority have more in common than they realize. Today's micro-chip is universal in its outreach, paying little regard to demarcation boundaries between persons or social groups. Modern unemployment, for example, is more wideranging than ever before – inter-regional, inter-generational, inter-social. The well-paid computer executive may well have an unemployed sister or daughter searching hard with her Arts Degree and Teaching Diploma for her first job. Indeed, the ranks of the contemporary unemployed constitute a social mix normally seen only in the conscription of wartime. This is another revolution of our times.

The media has also been a factor in generating national awareness. Programmes like *The Robots are Coming* have ensured that the chief agent of the new technology has become an international talking point. Humanity may not know *how* it is being got at by the 'chip', but it begins to appreciate that it *is* being got at. What needs now to be raised is the level of consciousness – an awareness that while we marvel at the skill, speed, cheapness, reliability and flexibility which characterize the new technology, we must at the same time appreciate the implications for the human race when these developments are taken in combination.

There are signs that society is beginning to take measure of what is going on particularly as new generations, less dependent on our outdated industrial culture, enter the debate. Though at government levels we lack an adequate response, something like a critical acceptance and appreciation is taking hold as up and down the country and across the world men and women begin to express their views in a language that is increasingly common. These people are in no doubt about the vastness of their task, but as Hazel Henderson, one of Schumacher's brilliant pupils has put it in a vision of ultimate hope which looks beyond the present difficulties:

> So as I have talked of breakdown and the exhaustion of industrial cultures I have tried also to celebrate what is being born: the overlooked shoots of a more benign technology, less materialistic goals, more holistic, reintegrated vision, a gentler metaphysic, a humbler, more realistic view of ourselves and an acceptance of our own finiteness and physical death.[15]

And in a superb reaffirmation of faith in ability of the human race to respond to challenge Henderson concludes:

> We humans are self-organizing systems, we do not have to tell our hearts when to beat. We have, in our collective history, also developed many examples of stable, self-organizing communities. This ability to self-organize is encoded in our DNA. We know how it could be – we have always known. We can now understand for the first time in our history, the teachings of our great spiritual leaders (who have always been the real futurists), the edict to serve the people, the values of love, caring, sharing, tolerance and humility.[16]

The 'invisible college', envisaged by Kenneth Boulding in his noble tract *The Meaning of the Twentieth Century*, is emerging as people of many countries and many cultures who have a vision of the transition through which we are passing devote their time and talents to contributing to its fulfilment. The members of this invisible college are not impractical dreamers but neither are they moved, like so many anti/Utopians, to retreat into intellectual despair leaving their less well-educated fellows to pick up the pieces. They have recognized their true role on this inter-dependent planet. They too have a vision of what is possible and are prepared to do what they can, where they can and when they can to make that vision come true.

And, what a gift awaits us if we have the wisdom to choose aright. The choice is awesome. It is magnificently put by Wassily Leontief, Nobel Prize Winner in Economics, in a borrowing of the Genesis story:

> Adam and Eve enjoyed, before they were expelled from Paradise, a high standard of living without working. After their expulsion they and their successors were condemned to eke out a miserable existence, working from dawn to dusk. The history of technological progress over the past two hundred years is essentially the story of the human species working its way slowly and steadily back into Paradise.
>
> What would happen, however, if we suddenly found ourselves in it? With all goods and services provided without work, no one would be gainfully employed. Being unemployed means receiving no wages. As a result, until appropriate new incomes policies were formulated to fit the changed technical conditions everyone would starve in Paradise.[17]

The contradiction is bizarre – yet for many it could (and has) become a fact of life. However, society can and must make choices. If we choose a covenant between man and machine based on the affirmation that men and women are God's creation, uniquely created for a divine purpose then all will be well. But if mammon is to be the centre of our moral gravity the nightmares of Huxley and Orwell will become our plight.

3

COMPULSORY AND COMPULSIVE WORK: GODS THAT FAIL

> 'I detested my work yet now that I'm paid-off I'm going half crazy. I used to think spare time would be marvellous; now I don't know where to begin' (former Midlands car worker).

There have always been those for whom work and a sense of fulfilment have been one – fortunate men and women for whom distinctions between work and leisure have been unimportant and from whose activities civilization has been enriched. In ancient Greece, for instance, leisure was viewed as a desirable end in itself and activities such as public service, scholarship, contemplation, and self-development were held in high esteem. Nearer our own time the privilege of self-realization through work has been in the main enjoyed by those who have had the advantage of wealth or status.

Bertrand Russell, who was himself an eminent member of this privileged group, described the system well in his *In Praise of Idleness*:

> In the past, there was a small leisure class and a larger working class. The leisure class enjoyed advantages for which there was no basis in social justice; this necessarily made it oppressive, limited its sympathies, and caused it to invent theories by which to justify its privileges. These facts greatly diminished its excellence, but in spite of this drawback it contributed nearly the whole of what we call civilization. It cultivated the arts and discovered the sciences; it wrote the books, invented the philosophies, and refined social relations. Even the liberation of the oppressed has usually been

> inaugurated from above. Without the leisure class, mankind would never have emerged from barbarism.[1]

But, as Russell would have been the first to admit, the system of a hereditary leisure class was extraordinarily wasteful and for every genius it produced there were legions of able people who were never given the opportunity to rise from their humble origins. For these, the labouring masses, work has been a burden to be endured – a necessary price to be paid for food, shelter and the other necessities of life.

Unfortunately philosophies of work have been little discussed from the point of view of those at 'the sharp end' of life and as a result a great many fanciful theories surround 'the labourer and his work' – romantic tales of honest toil abound, created in the main by writers who, however splendidly cultured, have lacked the special experience of *having* to depend on one's capacity to labour physically in order to obtain the bare necessities of life.

It has also been necessary for the industrial state to glorify work in order to maximize productivity and profit; so, the work ethic has been preached powerfully since the Industrial Revolution. It is still strong today, though the motive for working has for many changed from sheer survival reasons to urges which are basically social and psychological. Compulsory work is often replaced by compulsive labour.

But the challenge to traditional work assumptions is growing. Trade unionists – often among our most conservative upholders of the traditional system – are contributing to the debate. This, for instance, from Clive Jenkins and Barrie Sherman of the Scientific, Technical and Managerial Staffs Association:

> By and large people neither enjoy their work, nor do they enjoy travelling to and from it. Most jobs are repetitive, require little if any personal initiative and, for the most part, people are incapable of fulfilling anything like their full potential through them. . . People go to work that they do not enjoy, and spend a considerable proportion of their working hours getting to work and then getting home. It thus looms large in a life that is not very pleasant at the outset.[2]

Russell has been even more scathing in his criticism of those (including the Russians) who keep alive the notion that a great deal of heavy manual labour must be the lot of the average worker – rather than as a means to a state of affairs in which physically difficult and often degrading labour is no longer needed. Realist as he was, Bertrand Russell was in no doubt about the manual worker's approach to the job:

> If you ask him what he thinks is the best part of his life, he is not likely to say, 'I enjoy manual work because it makes me feel that I am fulfilling man's noblest task, and because I like to think how much man can transform his planet.' I have never heard working men say this sort of thing. They consider work, as it should be considered, a necessary means to a livelihood, and it is from their leisure hours that they derive whatever happiness they may enjoy.[3]

Russell's comment is not the whole story of why people work but for many it is an important part of the explanation. In addition, his view acts as a corrective to notions about the dignity of manual labour preached by those who have been careful to opt out of that particular 'uplifting' process.

The church has often added to misunderstanding about the nature of work and has done much to reinforce the Industrial Revolution work ethic. As a recent international symposium on 'Work and Religion' concluded, the Christian contribution to the subject has neglected to give due weight to the views of the protagonists of work, the workers, seen in their actual operations. Worse still, time is against the church:

> The modern theology of work attempts to give meaning to work precisely at a time when it appears to have become meaningless through industrialization.[4]

Professor Fiorenza's comment is a measure of the difficulties which the church faces in coming to grips with a new industrial order which is quite evidently emerging, though its outlines are still ill-defined. The 'Why work?' question has assumed a new urgency.

Research into motives and incentives among workers makes it clear that there is no *one* ideal incentive for work. Incentives vary from one culture to another, from one firm to another and from one individual to another leading to a hierarchy of satisfactions to do with companionship, status and personal fulfilment. It has also been noted that motives tend to become 'monetized': people have been taught that money is the key to satisfaction, so when they seek improvement they ask for more money.[5]

However, the range of the social researcher is most wide when it deals with choice work – for a large section of the working population (and especially in time of recession) no such choice is available. So while there may be no one ideal incentive, it is all too true that for most of our industrial history the reality of job selection for most people has been one of Hobson's choice. Money certainly becomes a lesser incentive when other incentives are realistically available, but until the point of real need has been met the money incentive greatly limits freedom to choose.

This 'sheer necessity' factor has been dominant from the inception of the Industrial Revolution and has greatly reduced job satisfaction. Writing during the first surges of industrialization in England Edmund Burke described the situation for industrial workers of his time as 'strange and ridiculous beyond expression', and talked of 'unhappy wretches . . . buried in the bowels of the earth . . . they work at a severe and dismal task, without the least prospect of being delivered from it'.[6]

Far removed from Burke in time and political outlook George Orwell's famous description of coal mining brings home the persistent unpleasantness and danger of heavy industry, notwithstanding a long line of Factory Acts and mechanical innovations:

> The time to go there is when the machines are roaring and the air is black with coal dust, and when you can actually see what the miners have to do. At those times the place is like hell, or at any rate like my own mental picture of hell. Most of the things one imagines in hell are there – heat, noise, confusion, darkness, foul air, and, above all, unbearably cramped space. Everything except the fire, for there is no fire down there except the feeble beams of Davy lamps and electric torches which scarcely penetrate the clouds of coal dust.[7]

Nearly fifty years later, on Christmas Eve 1982, the National Coal Board reported a sit-in at Kinneil colliery in Scotland when miners began a protest 3000 feet down in their pit against a planned closure decision by the Coal Board. NUM officials reported that the men were pledged to stay down as long as necessary so as to 'defend their jobs and those of their children and grandchildren.' The NCB had claimed that the pit was being closed for geological reasons.

But the fact of the matter is that few people would choose to work in such conditions (certainly not for a 5-day week) if reasonable alternatives were on offer. As often as not what is on offer is decidedly limited. My own experience of going to work in the Shipyard of Harland and Wolff in the 1940s was exactly that. The aim was to get into a trade – any trade – in order to avoid 'ending up a labourer'. Any refinements which one had in mind (but rarely got a chance to press – you took what was on offer) had to do with 'a steady job' and whether one went to the heavy 'black' trades (like drilling or caulking) or donned the brown overalls of the engineers (fitters, turners or electricians).

This has been a countrywide experience, as many interviews confirm. This from a 58-year old Bradford engineering worker is typical. He joined the trade in the 1930s and now looks forward to early retirement. When asked about why he took his first job he had this to say:

> There's an awful lot of theorizing about why people go to work, but for me and my generation there wasn't much to think about. In those days you were lucky to get any job when you left school and you were especially lucky if you had someone to 'speak' for you at the local works. I always liked books and was anxious to go on with my education, but by the time I was fourteen, and even though I passed every examination I sat, I knew what to expect. It was the local works for me because I had family there.
>
> My uncle 'spoke' for me and I was told to report for an apprenticeship. I wasn't even asked what I wanted to be. I just turned up one Monday morning at 7.30 with a bunch of other kids and we were distributed around the workshops. I'd hoped to be in the electrical shop, but I was told that that was full up so I'd have to be a fitter.
>
> But, you know, in those days we didn't expect more – if they'd put me to painting or joinery I'd still have thought myself lucky to have got into a trade. That's the way it was in the thirties. Things have improved a good deal with job counselling and so on, but make no mistake about it, for most kids there's still a great deal of chance in the first job. A lot depends on where you live, and who you know, especially when things are slack.
>
> I often wonder where I'd have ended up if I'd been able to

> continue my schooling. I've never really liked working with my hands – I think I'd have liked to have been a librarian.

This yearning for something better is one of the burdens which often accompanies compulsory work – the loss to society is great and the frustration felt by the labour force considerable. The point was well-illustrated in a discussion with a 55-year old housewife, mother to three graduate sons, who told me in an interview about her entry into working life:

> The work we do is a very important part of our lives; yet we are haphazard about it.
>
> I always knew what I wanted to be – I wanted to teach and my old schoolmaster encouraged me and several others in our ambitions. But in those days it was useless. I passed the entrance exam to grammar school with flying colours, but my widowed mother couldn't afford the supplementary fees so, like a good many of my elementary school friends, it was a case of putting 'grand ideas' behind me and looking for a job at fourteen. I managed to avoid the mill and got into the making-up trade as a stitcher and there I remained until I married in my early twenties, working at the machine all day and often bringing pieces home at night to fold so as to get ahead on bonus work next day.
>
> If it hadn't been for evening classes, the WEA, local church and trade union I think I'd have gone mad with the sheer boredom of it all. That's what I think was worst of all, the repetition – though often the work was so routine that we were able to get on with our conversations. At times I think we didn't notice the work and got on with our personal relationships – and they were a good bunch who stuck by one another through thick and thin.
>
> But how I missed my school and the books. I wonder now where all those bright kids I played with have gone; and what a debt we owe to the teachers of those days, though it must have been heart-breaking for them to raise expectations in us which they knew couldn't be fulfilled.

There is an interesting ending to this story. The lady in question discovered the Open University in her forties; now a graduate, she combines her home-making with her chosen career of teaching. But she is an exception to the rule which governed her generation in the job selection process.

The above examples are taken from the fairly recent past, but for working people the 'first job' experience has changed little down the centuries. What information we have from earlier days underlines the point that the working classes (the great majority of the nation) have been rarely in control of their working destiny.

John Burnett in his fascinating collection of working-class autobiographies gives us a vivid behind-the-scenes glimpse of reality. We learn of a patient resignation to the facts of life, combined with the feeling that human existence is a struggle and that survival is an end in itself:

> Such resignation was, in part, the product of a long history of deprivation and suffering by which, for generations past, working people had been accustomed to poverty, personal tragedy and limited expectations; for some it was reinforced by the religious teaching that the world was, in any case, a vale of tears and that happiness could only be expected in the life to come.[8]

Some workers, of course, have found a great deal of satisfaction beyond money in their jobs; skilled hand-workers with pride in their products and farm labourers with a love for their animals are cases in point, but the evidence collected by Burnett and others indicates that work has been regarded by the working classes as a means to an end and not an end in itself. Certainly the recorded views of the factory hands in sweated trades, domestic servants and navvies indicate that they did not philosophize about their toil or demand a sense of fulfilment from it.

What is also clear from Burnett's collection of autobiographies is that work for most was taken as a grim fact like life itself, to be endured rather than enjoyed. Most were glad to have any kind of paid employment (reminiscent of today's much heard comment, 'Well, it's a job anyway, and you're lucky to have one') and to expect to derive satisfaction or happiness from it was an irrelevant consideration. This is not to say that personal relationships on the job did not matter – as a present generation knowledgeable about *Upstairs, Downstairs* will recognize, such relationships *did* matter – but at the point of entry into a job the 'hierarchy of satisfaction' was not a subject for consideration and after entry it had a very limited application.

And as the record shows, even those workers who were intellectually well-endowed had to take whatever was available. Winifred

Foley (b. 1914), who eventually won success as a writer, describes her reaction as the day for entry into domestic service drew nearer:

> Like the sword of Damocles my fourteenth birthday approached to cut me in half. My spirit to remain with everything familiar that I knew and loved and the reluctant rest of me to go into domestic service. This was the common lot of every girl in our mining village, unless she were too mentally or physically handicapped, and I had grown up with this knowledge. Now the time had come, I found it hard to bear.
>
> Now I was to be parted from my family, my friends, my home, the school, the village – all that I loved most dearly. To them, too, I was a person, but I knew from hearsay that once I donned the maid's cap and apron I would become a menial, a nobody, mindful of my place on the bottom shelf.[9]

But there was no alternative open to the poor and as one of Winifred Foley's companions who had also had to turn down a won place in the grammar school put it, 'Money alone was the key to success.'

A recent eighty-fifth birthday interview with Sir Sacheverell Sitwell was delightfully revealing on this point. Sir Sacheverell, when asked about his success, had this to say:

> I have been frightfully lucky to have a small private income. A private income is so important – not too big a one, otherwise you will never do any work will you?

The Times commented:

> He has done his work. He has been everywhere, seen everything. Sir Sachie, whatever the critical reception of his 80 books may have been, admits to having had the most frightfully good time. And that, it may be argued, is the greatest aesthetic achievement of all.[10]

Money may not be the only key to job satisfaction and choice of career, but it helps.

Happy too at their work are those with a rare talent which finds an outlet – their satisfaction is great and society is the richer for their contribution. Another octogenarian, Sir Ralph Richardson, recently gave his testimony:

> In my life I have had the great good luck to work on a job I respect

> deeply, the drama, and in all its branches, theatre, films and television. Among these branches I have spent more than sixty years in a magnetic forest.
>
> And the forest is growing all the time. I have seen it grow in my time: wonderful things have happened, new seeds have blown in and made it quite different . . . it is beautiful.[11]

As the move away from compulsory labour to choice work gathers momentum, the prospect of a society offering a new dimension of creativity opens up and a new and more human person-to-person relationship becomes possible as the need for competition in material matters recedes. Few would be following in the literary footsteps of a Sitwell or would be able to vie with Sir Ralph in his dramatic performances, but it is equally certain that a vast new range of options for human development could become a practical reality.

Herbert Marcuse's prediction of a progressive reduction of traditional labour will be fulfilled. So more profound questions arise: can the system provide for occupation without what we now know as work; more important, and more difficult, can it develop needs which transcend the market economy and may even be incompatible with it?[12]

Such a change in life role involving millions is already under way: comprehensive, fast moving, unstoppable. We are in the midst of a revolution that will count as one of the most momenteous in the history of human society. Given inspiration and sound direction, that revolution could make possible the hope of a previous generation:

> The human spirit, freed at last from its immemorial bondage to material cares, might display for the first time all the splendour of which it is capable.[13]

4

PROFILE OF THOSE IN SPECIAL NEED: UB40 PEOPLE

> 'I get terribly depressed. Sometimes I think I'll finish it all, but I haven't the nerve' (Witness at Manpower Services Commission Inquiry into Unemployment).

UB40 is the name of a popular pop group, but it is also a sign of growing segregation – it is the code name for the Registration Card given to those who 'sign on' as unemployed at the Social Security Office. As such, with its basic information about the holder, it has become our best known natural identification card, and is much relied on by the police as an 'ID'. Many card holders are convinced that they are branded for life – the 'Giro (benefit) generation', or 'Giro fusiliers' as those who depend on Social Security benefits are known in some parts of the country. Others talk of the 'R' label: retired, redundant, re-deployed, rationalized and, worst of all, rejected.[1]

The quotation which heads this chapter conveys some of the doom-laden feeling which characterizes a good deal of contemporary unemployment – 'Britain's placid jobless' as one economist has described them. This reaction is in marked contrast to previous decades when the attitude was one of 'waiting for trade to pick up again'. Now it is different: deep down, many believe that there is no trade left in which the 'picking-up' can take place. 'My job is gone forever' – that is the chilling comment heard in working-class clubs throughout the land. These are the people on whom the burden of UB40 lies heaviest. So emerges an especially vulnerable group in society for whom provision must be made. They are a large and growing section of the nation who, through no fault of their own, have become casualties in the process of industrial reorganization which the government on behalf of the nation is pursuing.

If it is necessary that millions should be excluded from the production process so that production may be improved, surely it is morally indefensible that this large minority should be asked to bear a disproportionate share of the cost of that reorganization. What is needed is a recognition that we are one people and that the unemployed are entitled to full citizenship. But clearly the application of that principle will require from the rest of the community a willingness to share with and care for their unemployed brothers and sisters. Such an attitude is not only morally just; it is a social and economic imperative.

As a Resolution of the Council of Europe has put it:

> The success of measures against unemployment will depend largely on the achievement of a social consensus which requires sincere solidarity on the part of everyone in employment, in particular in the framework of negotiations between management and labour which should be conducted in a spirit of collective responsibility towards their 'third partner', those who are unemployed.[2]

Yet there are no clear signs that the nation has awakened to the full plight of our 'third partner' or of the national reassessment required. Certainly there is no movement in opinion similar to the wartime stirrings which led to the appointment of the Beveridge Inquiry and the consequent national commitment to build the Welfare State.

No doubt there is a good deal of public sympathy with the unemployed, but mingled with the sympathy there is also a feeling that redundancy is a risk which all who join in the economic struggle must face – a private grief to bear. Charity is certainly offered to those in need, but there is much less public concern about the deep-seated causes of unemployment; we are learning that a philosophy of fair shares is as difficult to propagate in an affluent society as it is in one of scarcity.

Much of this ambiguity has to do with the fact that we live in a situation where the work ethic is drummed into us from childhood. Work is declared to be a moral duty, with those who do not labour being exposed to public censure (though there are contradictions: many with inherited wealth live lives of leisure yet escape criticism). So the myths abound. 'Scroungers', 'work shy' and 'dole fiddlers' –

all 'getting their arms into the community'. However, the chronic unemployed are not without their advocates. Influential groups are increasingly challenging the conventional wisdom that economic growth will automatically result in a corresponding growth of jobs. The 'neither work nor want' jibe is being replaced by the 'want to work but cannot' truth.

A 'special case' argument for the new unemployed is being heard – and, encouragingly, across the traditional political divide. The House of Lords, for instance, has provided some of the most incisive comment. A massive 1981 all-party Report looked at the cause and nature of unemployment and was able to offer virtually unanimous recommendations. The conclusion reached was clear:

> We regard the existence of over three million unemployed as an affront, a prodigal waste of human resources, the source of much personal misery and a stumbling-block in the way of prosperity.

And this, from Lord Carr of Hadley, an eminent member of the CBI, taking us to the heart of the matter by identifying and underlining two general but fundamental propositions which are contained in the Lords Report:

> First, the primary and only permanent remedy for our present deplorable state of unemployment is to make British industry more competitive. The second general but fundamental proposition is that the present level of unemployment is intolerable. It is not just deplorable; it is intolerable.

What is significant is that Lord Carr, a pillar of the industrial establishment, goes on to stress the need for action on *both* fronts:

> The long-term remedy of improving competitiveness should be partnered with measures of more immediate effect. Partnering long term remedy with shorter term measures seems to be the main argument and conclusion of the Committee which the government, at least by implication, reject.

And in a recognition of the need for natural unity we are reminded:

> It is not just of humanitarian necessity to do something more quickly but it is, in view of this non-partisan, all-party committee, a necessity in order to win that measure of general consent and support that is necessary to carry through what is a long pro-

> gramme of recovery, which is bound to be painful and one in which many people are bound to suffer in the short run.[3]

But it is not only the government which shows signs of unsureness as long-term unemployment rises. Many in the nation seem quite prepared to take the view that 'we have to live with the problem' – that is, so long as someone else has to do the living. In fact, as one survey into public attitudes puts it:

> A kind of public 'schizophrenia' has developed where, as concern mounts with rising levels of unemployment there is strong criticism of the workless as individuals: the workless tend to be viewed as worthless. The workers are seen as expendable and, as a result, it is now confidently argued that government intervention to lower the level of unemployment is neither possible nor desirable. Unemployment, if not an act of God, has come to be seen as the act of the god in the economic machine.[4]

Proof, if proof were needed, that the 'affluent society' and the 'indifferent society' are never far apart.

The people of the poverty trap

David Sheppard has recently alerted Christians to the danger of indifference to the 'losers in the urban race'. This pastor to the poor faces the facts of poverty every day in Liverpool and speaks from a situation where it is a luxury to ask questions about the quality of work: 'any job seems like a blessing'.[5] Unfortunately Liverpool is only one of a growing number of urban areas that are being blighted by the special poverty which accompanies long-term unemployment. In these areas, in disproportionate numbers, live those who are caught in the poverty trap – at the bottom of the social ranking, more likely to be unskilled, low in income, older and less fit. To add to their difficulty, in periods of economic depression the position of these groups is worsened by pressure on lower skill jobs from better qualified redundant work seekers. Indeed, one of the signs of our ill-divided industrial world is that while the highly-skilled are protected in their monopolies by strict trade union rules no such protection extends to the mass of the 'unskilled' market – in that market there is a permanent open season. So in times of economic contraction the poor become poorer. Is it any wonder that David Sheppard's 'losers' are glad of any job?

Low wages

But even when employment *is* available the 'losers' find themselves in jobs which do little to improve their standard of living. Studies into transmitted deprivation show that for many workers there is no compensation in the labour market (sometimes quite the reverse) and it remains one of the harsh paradoxes of economic life that the most unpleasant jobs are often the worst paid. Conditions of service in terms of health hazards, holidays and hours of work are also unattractive.[6] Nor is it sufficiently appreciated how vast and how permanent the labouring poor have become as a group. The 1982 National Health dispute highlighted the problem, but as reports by the independent Low Pay Unit reveal health workers are not alone in their grievance.

It is reckoned that about seven million adults, nearly one-third of the work force are low paid, using the widely-accepted definition of low pay as two-thirds of the average male wage, equivalent to about £90 per week. In fact, low pay is now recognized as an important cause of poverty in Britain. Nearly a quarter of the two million people living below the official poverty line in 1979 were in families with at least one full-time worker. It is also estimated that the number in poverty would quadruple to eight million without the contribution of increased women's earnings to family budgets.

Some idea of the extent of this deprivation is indicated in an official table published in April 1982:

Occupation (full-time)	Average gross weekly earnings (£)	% earning below £100
Women		
Hairdressers	56.00	98.7
Barmaids	65.90	93.8
Waitresses	66.40	92.4
Saleswomen, shop assistants, shelf fillers	66.60	96.2
Kitchen hands	67.90	91.1
Retail shop check out operators	69.60	94.4
Sewing machinists (textiles)	71.50	91.4
Receptionists	72.30	91.0
Counter hands	72.30	91.0
Cleaners	73.70	89.7

Men		
Barmen	94.60	62.3
General farm workers	95.10	65.5
Road sweepers	97.20	68.7
Butchers, meat cutters	98.00	62.1
Gardeners/groundsmen (non domestic)	100.70	55.4
Caretakers	101.60	51.5
Hospital porters	102.20	51.5
Salesmen, shop assistants, shelf fillers	102.60	59.8
Agricultural machinery drivers/operators	102.70	53.1
Cleaners	104.30	53.7

Source: New Earnings Survey, Department of Employment, April 1982.

In addition, the deprived groups are also among the least well organized for collective bargaining, with union links that are much more tenuous than those enjoyed by skilled workers (and all too often union benefits and responsibilities end with the cessation of employment – herein lies a challenge of adaptation for the trade union movement). A letter in the *Daily Mail* of 15 December 1982 makes the point:

> As one of the 3½ million on the scrapheap, I feel qualified to comment on Geoffrey Goodman's article, 'Silent Army of Despair'.
>
> How can the unemployed speak up when they have no one to represent them?
>
> Many of us were once union members – I was a shop steward for many years. But from the attitude of the big Unions you would think the unemployed do not exist any more.

In view of the range of useful (often vital) services covered by the 'unskilled' it is clear that the rest of society takes advantage of their apparent inability to press their industrial demands. In recent years evidence has been growing that the tide may be turning as in a succession of strikes the 'under people' of industry and in the public services have begun to sense their potential strength. This is no idle threat. Many of those who strike in wage-leading industries have very little real 'muscle' in terms of public inconvenience, compared to the essential services offered by those who work for little reward in the sewage, garbage and other equally essential but highly unpleasant sectors of industry. When this fact sinks home determined leadership will use the hidden bargaining power of the underprivileged to bring more justice into the unfair world of reward differentials. As it is, the present pattern of wage and salary determination is a jungle of anomalies in which prestige occupations are often able to project themselves as more important to society than they really are. Too often rewards bear little relation to the value of the job being done. Those who operate in economically sheltered sectors are placed in a strong bargaining position; and those who threaten economic 'clout' enjoy equal benefits in the wage and salary league. In such circumstances those who do not *have* 'clout' or who do not wish to use it against the public are at a distinct disadvantage.

A system of hidden 'clout' based on subtle social conventions also operates, ensuring that top-pay groups are 'suitably' rewarded. Such categories are distinctly fortunate in that their claims are considered by arbitrators who are themselves, by education and class, likely to accept the assumptions on which top pay claims are based. The lower paid do not enjoy this social kinship. So it happens, the most lowly paid in the nation are asked to have regard to the national interest (as in the case of many Health Service workers living near the frontiers of poverty) while the immeasurably better off are much more generously treated. Percentage increases add to the unequality.

Unfair differentials are among the most divisive forces in modern industrial society. They are controversial in the extreme, raising fundamental questions about basic assumptions to do with class and work values. Certainly, not nearly enough weight is given to the fact that unlike those who do menial work (and 'menial' in itself begs a good many questions) top pay occupations enjoy great rewards in job satisfaction and social cache. Such 'in-service' dividends are difficult to quantify, but they are real and should be more taken into account when pay comparisons are made with those at the bottom of the earnings league and for whom talk of job satisfaction may have little meaning. Total reward, rather than cash return, should be the overall consideration.

What is socially weakening – and often morally indefensible – about the present position is that it breeds cynicism among those caught up in heavy or unpleasant labour. It also breeds what former rail union leader Sid Weighell called 'the philosophy of the pig trough'. Such cynicism is powerfully fuelled when we are able to read in *The Times* (9.7.81) that the distinction of being the highest paid executive in Britain, at a rate of £300,000 per annum, went to the head of the Playboy organization. Sometime later (28.10.82) the Bradford correspondent of that paper was reporting on what they believed to be Britain's lowest paid 55-year-old worker at a wage of £27.27, whose income was to be doubled after an agreement negotiated by the trade union.

The extent of poverty

Unfortunately for many millions of the working poor depressed earnings, while a fundamental aspect of their plight, are also part of a wider nexus of depriving conditions to do with low status employment. The 1982 Department of Health and Social Security sponsored study into Deprivation and Disadvantage offers a rich quantity of facts and conclusions for those who require evidence of considerable deprivation in Britain. In the words of Norman Fowler, Secretary of State for Social Services:

> As these findings show, deprivation and disadvantage are not just concepts. They are a reality; and they persist despite changes in social policy which were intended to eliminate them and despite very broadly based improvements in the living standards of most people.[7]

For those commentators who believe that the poor have only themselves to blame, this latest picture of Britain's underprivileged may give cause to think again. Even allowing for the fact that there have been many improvements in living standards over this century, and granting that in no sense does poverty nowadays mean the same as it did a generation ago, it is clear that certain groups and areas of the country are more vulnerable than others to deprivation. The DHSS survey believes that on a conservative estimate roughly ten million people are suffering from poverty, over four million of them in families with children. About a quarter of the work force hold unskilled or semi-skilled jobs, with attendant difficulties of insecurity and poor work conditions, while three million are currently unemployed and 1.8 million households are living in physically unsatisfactory conditions in terms of overcrowding, shortage of amenities or general unfitness, and a small minority, about fifty thousand, are received as officially homeless in any one year. It is also noted that ethnic minorities are as groups especially at risk, as are large families and single parent families.

Of course, estimates of the number of people living on low incomes depend on the definition of poverty and how it is measured. 'But if a poverty line based on Supplementary Benefit is adopted, it would seem that around a quarter of the population in Britain are in households in poverty or relatively close to it, i.e., with an income at or below 140% of the Supplementary Benefit rate.' No doubt measurements of social deprivation are both inexact and controversial, and it is also clear that crude figures can underestimate as well as overestimate the prevalence of deprivation. But what cannot be doubted is that the disparate collection of figures amassed over a ten-year research period 'show deprivation to be quite definitely substantial in amount.'[8]

The massive group encompassed by these conclusions are precisely those who are most in danger of becoming permanent casualties of the reorganization process dictated by technical innovation. And (as many are already finding a difficult fact of life) it is not easy for those caught in what is feared as permanent unemployment to create a tolerable alternative life-style. I recall a barbed comment from a recent Union conference on unemployment: 'If they cannot have work, let them enjoy "leisure".' It was a grim jest containing within it a host of anxieties and transition perplexities. As one 50-year old printer put it to me: 'Do they think we are all budding Jimmy Galway's or Duncan Goodhew's, wanting to whistle or swim all day long? When are our armchair philosophers going to learn that we need real work and need it now?'

The medical dimension

It is becoming clear that many of those for whom leisure time is becoming available may be least able to adapt to the opportunity because of the physical and psychological effects which often accompany job loss. In particular (and to return to an earlier theme) for those for whom *compulsory* work has become a *compulsive* need the prospect of long-term unemployment is likely to produce alarming withdrawal symptoms. These symptoms have become well known in medical circles and, as the 1982 British Association heard, there is now overwhelming evidence that persistent unemployment causes stress which in turn creates ill-health.

Nor is it only the poorest sections of society who feel undervalued. Increasingly, well-educated people find themselves unable to use the educational qualifications on which they have built up career expectations. Writing to *The Observer* in September 1982, one such had this to say:

> As a BA in Eng. Lit., currently employed as a receptionist on £53 a week after tax, I was amused and also a little irritated to read your Student Service column last week which enthused over the career value of a University Arts education. I was amused because its arguments were, idea for idea, almost exactly those put to myself and fellow pupils by our grammar school headmaster.
>
> I was irritated because, like him, you gave so little emphasis to the other side of the story – the difficulties when it comes to real life, of extracting any actual use or gain, careerwise, from the three years. I would hate to see another generation conned by nebulous promise, coming painfully to the same conclusion.

A sad letter which raises many questions about how we are to motivate our young people.

The psychological shock experienced by those who are unemployed or underemployed can be greatly lessened by the possession of a strong faith and the support of companions who share that faith. Elaine Brown in her personal diary *Grounded* tells how the bottom can drop out of a middle-class world when the head of the family loses his job – John Brown, who had been used to sitting at the controls of an airliner, found himself at 47 with no flying job and having to do with spells of labouring work. At such times more than traditional 'bread and butter' welfare is necessary. Elaine Brown stresses the importance of her Christian connection:

> I am beginning to see that this trust in God is what matters most of all, much more than even the solving of our unemployment problem – though this too will one day come to an end. And meanwhile, faith in God's complete rightness can enable us to live without the thing we've longed and hoped for. If we place our hand deliberately in his we are safe – whatever.[9]

But Elaine Brown's spiritual strength is by no means universally enjoyed – and in many respects the church has not got its message over (and is also unsure of what that message *is*) to those who feel threatened by contemporary industrial society. So, as in other departments of life, the urban poor feel required to 'go it alone' in a process of adaptation which challenges the assumptions of a lifetime.

Clearly the mental and physical suffering associated with long-term unemployment is considerable and it is recognized by the medical profession that the various forms of pathology which accompany unemployment are of increasing social significance. The British Medical Journal has published regional findings from doctors with day-to-day experience of dealing with unemployed patients and all agree that work is conducive to mental and physical health and that protracted periods of unemployment may increase the risk of morbidity and mortality. Indeed the medical world is increasingly of one opinion that loss of work is a major life event which requires adaptation and is inherently stressful.[10]

The medical world has responded to this new threat to health by making efforts to pool information and to encourage a national response among the profession. For example, at the 1981 BMA Symposium at Southampton on the hazards of unemployment, delegates were warned that though the link between unemployment and physical/social ill effects is obvious, 'the strength of the effects may not be widely enough recognized'.

Important reaction stages have been noted by doctors: the initial shock and disbelief combined with optimism and a sense of being on holiday; then the holiday feeling gives way to meaningless leisure, inertia and exhaustion, with a loss of self-esteem and tensions in the family; and lastly, the 'broken state', in which despite the lifting of earlier anxiety and depression, there is a feeling of inferiority, submissiveness, and inability to provide for needs, with acceptance of the new 'non-occupational' identity, a more limited way of life, and little hope of change. Professor W. Linford Rees, who has done pioneer work on the medical aspects of unemployment, calls for a plan of action by his profession based on four important initiatives:

> Firstly, full-scale prospective longitudinal studies should be started to define the psychological and physical hazards of unemployment more precisely and find ways of obviating them and to identify high risk groups.
>
> Secondly, counselling and guidance services should be provided for the unemployed and those due to be made redundant, to help them to use their time more effectively and to maintain their morale.
>
> Thirdly, programmes of job creation and training are needed for all grades of work.
>
> Finally, doctors and social workers should be alert to the adverse effects of unemployment both on the unemployed person

and on the family, and general practitioners, in particular, should be on the outlook for anxiety and depressive states.'

And in an eminently practical call to the medical profession, which has a ring of 'bias to the poor' about it:

> Now is the time for doing these things, not in some hoped-for, more affluent future. Though special programmes, services, and studies would be ideal, it should not go beyond the ingenuity of doctors and others both to provide more informal help and to start collecting information as opportunity offers.[11]

These practical recommendations and conclusions are encouraging evidence of how one important professional group is taking delivery of unemployment consequences which are its specialist concern. But more than that the action proposed is an example of the way in which alert professional groups, while dealing with technical problems within their professional competence, can take part also in the wider debate and so promote community action without which narrower remedies may be merely palliative in effect.[12]

Why the new poor are a special case

The main thrust of this chapter has been to argue that 'special case' treatment must be accorded to those who are being trapped in long term unemployment. In summary, there is a three-fold justification:

1. Economically – because the poor are locked in a nexus of material disabilities from which by their own efforts they cannot escape. Society has spent vast fortunes creating the productivity conditions which in large part accounts for this situation; it is only fair that we should as a nation be equally conscious of the need to respond effectively to the urgent needs of those who are being 'dispensed' with. Colin Bedford has said it all with his plea for immediate help: 'This is a cry from the inner city to the decision-takers to listen before it is too late.'[13]

2. Socially – the millions involved in chronic unemployment are a vital part of the nation. Harnassed, they provide a valuable natural asset; rejected, they have an explosive potential which could make many of our inner cities 'no go' areas.

3. Morally – here the case for special category status is strongest. There is no way in which those without employment can be blamed

for their plight; they are victims of change. The point has been put forcefully by the Professor of Social Policy at Edinburgh University:

> Economists and public policy makers debate the question: how much unemployment can the country stand? Strictly speaking it is not 'the country' that is being asked to 'stand unemployment'.
>
> Unemployment does not, like air pollution or God's gentler rain, fall uniformly upon everyone . . . it strikes from underneath, it strikes particularly at those at the bottom of our society.[14]

In our society compensation for loss of property rights is freely given when it is deemed necessary for the public good that such rights must be given up. Yet for many of our poorest citizens the only 'property' they have to sell is their labour – it is a strange form of justice that asks them to sacrifice, sometimes for ever, this their most precious possession in pursuit of a national economic policy. Oddly enough, when generous compensation for loss of employment *is* offered it frequently goes to those who are professionally well-qualified and consequently in possession of a high degree of job mobility which greatly facilitates their re-employment. So, often, this latter category receives the 'golden handshake' *and* the opportunity of alternative work – a greatly diminished 'hardship'.

But for the urban poor, just *being* unemployed is sacrifice enough. It is little wonder that those who speak for the blighted areas call for a national commitment which will give their people (particularly the young and non-academic) a feeling that they matter, environmental and building programmes that will replace the lonely existing derelict sites which dominate the landscapes of the poor, welfare amenities geared to local needs and leisure facilities in line with the needs and means of those who require them most. Most important of all is an administrative back-up, in close co-operation with local community groups underpinned by firm and long-term guarantees from Government.

The inner city riots of recent years have alerted politicians of all parties to the special needs of the urban poor. We are confronted by a national issue calling for a bi-partisan approach. Is it too much to hope for a national response to help those who are caught up in a problem which they can barely comprehend and which they are incapable of solving from their own resources? A raising of our natural sights is called for. We are in need of the authority and imagination of a new Beveridge Plan.

5

A ROLE FOR THE CHURCH

> 'The church has a special obligation to speak on behalf of the vulnerable and the inarticulate and those whose bargaining power in society is weak' (Robert Runcie).

Any call for a natural crusade on behalf of those who are front line casualties in a new industrial revolution would be powerfully stimulated if the church could become a catalyst for such a campaign.

The church is well placed to be such a pressure group – straddling as it does the whole spectrum of the community it can be a unique lobby articulating the Christian social demand and encouraging its people to discover and apply their application of such demands through national and local church initiatives. The international outreach of the church is equally impressive.

In human resources alone the church has on call a range of practical skills and intellectual abilities possessed by few other institutions. The fact that this reservoir of talent can so often be drawn on virtually free of charge is an inestimable gift in an increasingly cost conscious world.

Some idea of what is available is reflected in the statistics of the 1983 UK Christian Handbook. The latest report indicates a church that has considerable strength in numbers and variety of social spread. It has a significance of outreach equalled by few institutions in society. Adult church membership is 17.4%, with a once-a-month attendance rate of one in seven of the adult population. As Philip Morgan, General Secretary of the British Council of Churches observes: 'The general picture which is presented is one of a quiet ferment of active life, sustaining well established and traditional patterns of service and witness and ready to experiment in new ways.'[1]

The resources which represent Philip Morgan's 'quiet ferment' are impressive. Some 25,000 full-time staff (and many more voluntary and part-timers) serve the various church agencies with a financial income of £350 million per annum. It is also interesting to note the communications potential of the church. With a total Christian membership organized through 51,000 churches and served by 45,000 ministers, the contact with people is considerable and so too is the opportunity to promote a national dialogue and to be an opinion-maker. The congregational contact is greatly strengthened by the growing communications network available to the church. In printed material alone the growth has been startling in recent years. Published each year are 76,000,000 copies of 390 magazines and 25,000,000 copies of newspapers. The church bookshop movement continues to expand and new developments in film and video together with the use of radio theatre and other art forms add greatly to the communications potential.

Properly used, such a potential could be a powerful force in national discussions about the future shape of our society. If it is not used, what other pressure group will fill the gap?

But it is not easy to harnass church membership to social action causes. Many Christians have doubts about what the role of the church should be in such matters. In the present century a line of distinguished teachers have tried to meet their objections. Most distinguished and most in touch with the honest fears of his people, Archbishop William Temple was a guide to social responsibility matters for a former generation and his influence is still with us. We are particularly indebted to him for the way in which he urged a discovery of the place of Christian social action in our own lives. He also made it clear that the claim (and responsibility) of the church to be heard in relation to political and economic problems was no new usurpation, but a reassertion of a right once universally admitted and widely regarded. The 'contracting-out' theory was 'entirely modern and extremely questionable'. So as far as the church was concerned: 'It is bound to "interfere" because it is by vocation the agent of God's purpose, outside the scope of which no human interest or activity can fall.'[2]

Temple was well aware that the church was likely to be attacked from both sides when it did its public duty and he knew that his call for the Christian church to make its voice heard in matters of politics and economics was widely resented, even by those who were

Christian in personal belief and devotional practice. But there was no alternative for the church: 'If it is faithful to its Commission it will ignore both sets of complaints, and continue so far as it can to influence all citizens and permeate all parties.'[3]

In his *Christianity and the Social Order* Temple presented a guide to action which in clarity and influence has never been bettered; more than any other church leader he confronted British Christians with the possibility of rebuilding the shattered social teaching of the church and brought to the fore the need to make social questions subject to Christian morality and especially to the doctrine of the dignity and importance of the individual. His advice is still valid as we face the challenges of a new industrial order:

> The method of the church's impact upon society at large should be two-fold. The church must announce Christian principles and point out where the existing social order at any time is in conflict with them. It must then pass on to Christian citizens, acting in their civic capacity, the task of reshaping the existing social order in conformity to the principles.[4]

At this point technical knowledge may be required and judgments of practical expediency will arise. If, for example, a bridge is to be built, the church may remind the engineer that he has an obligation to build a really safe bridge; but it is not entitled to make judgments about his design arrangements. So, in just the same way, Temple concludes, the church may tell the politician what ends the social order should promote; but it must leave to the politician the devising of the precise means to those ends.

For principles on which we can base our actions in practical situations we are offered: 'Freedom, Fellowship, Service – these are the three principles of a Christian social order, derived from the still more fundamental Christian postulates that man is a child of god and is destined for a life of eternal fellowship with Him.'[5]

But not even Temple can give the gift of certainty in political specifics. Nor would he have wanted to: 'The church is committed to the everlasting Gospel and to the creeds which formulate it; it must never commit itself to an ephemeral programme of detailed action.'[6]

It is no new thing for Christians to be concerned about public issues. Indeed as William Neil once observed, 'keeping politics out of the pulpit' was the last thing any of the early prophets ever dreamt of doing:

> All of them claimed to be speaking on behalf of God, and none of them regarded the faith of Israel as a meditative pursuit to be engaged in within the cloister or the study but as something to be proclaimed, defended and fought for in the political and social stresses of his day.[7]

The debate has moved on a great deal since Archbishop Temple's time and even among evangelicals there is growing acknowledgment of the biblical imperatives of social concern and action. The concern has come late in the day and one can readily agree with David Wright's assessment that

> It would be difficult to refute the charge that the evangelical quest for heaven has too often been attended by a devaluation of the welfare and just ordering of man's earthly life, a failure to accord proper weight to our thinking and priorities to the world of God's creation; Although the importance of social involvement has been regularly acknowledged, it has somehow rarely seemed important enough to engage more than marginal commitment. Evangelical ethics have for the most part been content to be personal rather than social.[8]

David Wright is hopeful as he welcomes evangelical mariners into, for them, largely uncharted waters. If he is also correct in his assessment that the new commitment represents 'the seal on an evangelical conversion' then we can hope for a oneness of action among Christians as we reflect on the biblical basis, the gospel basis and the socio-economic-political basis for social ethics.[9]

John Stott, who has been at the heart of this debate, lends his great authority in calling for evangelicals to be involved in social action and to go beyond words to concrete measures. He admits that his people have much catching up to do and that the backlog of work is enormous. Admitting that many of today's complex questions have no glib, easy or even sure answers, Stott warns his people 'not to be content to remain for ever in a state of suspended animation'; nor is it enough to produce 'biblical scholars rather than creative thinkers'.

And in a call to go beyond words to action:

> All of us will agree that theological reflection is indispensable to translate our theology into action. Knowledge of scripture can never be an end in itself. We are called not only to 'believe' the truth, but to 'do' or 'obey' it. Yes, we need evangelical dreamers as well as evangelical thinkers, who will dream their dreams of a better world, until their hearts burn within them and they go out and do something.[10]

Reaching the poor

John Stott's people could put new vigour into the movement of those who seek to reach the poor, but, as he would be the first to acknowledge, his appeal for Christians to 'go out and do something' is easier said than done. In many inner city areas it is a case of beginning from the ground up. To quote again from the Liverpool situation:

> It is impossible to exaggerate the gap between very large numbers of urban working-class people and the organized church. If that gap is to be bridged, there need to be many stepping stones, events, groups, projects in which those outside the church can meet with members of the Christian community. This is not to deny our calling to name the name of Christ. We may need to understand that the gap is so great that for some people it will take a generation to bridge it.[11]

Stark news indeed, and not unique to Liverpool.

It is all too clear that it is not easy for the church to participate effectively in the inner city. The problems of even 'hearing' the deprived are considerable. Today's poor speak in social 'tongues' which the church does not easily understand. Also, urban missionaries are thin on the ground and rarely get the priority in provision which their role merits.

As those who work among the urban poor affirm, they struggle within a framework of sheer loneliness, dealing with a tide of social problems which returns as quickly as it is thrust back. This situation is not inevitable – it is a by-product of the way in which the church goes about its business.

Indeed one of the contradictions about church mission effort at home is that as the need for the application of greater resources increases (*and* as the opportunity for evangelization also increases) so there is a tendency for the full-time ministry and other agents of church action to decline (though of course, the vast 'informal economy' of the church is an ever-present, but not always used, bonus).

But *can* the church put its money where its heart should be? Clearly if this is to be done the church's decision makers must grasp 'nettles' – nettles to do with church finances, with capital investment in underdeveloped parishes, and with the deployment of human resources to ensure that the talent of the ministry is spread in accordance with the mission needs of our time. In many down-town churches 'the lights go out' when the service is over with worshippers departing for their suburban homes. So the ever-open-door tradition of the church is eroded and the impression of the church as a Sunday-only institution is underlined.

But there are alternatives. For example, many churches have found an answer by converting their buildings into multi-purpose areas for Christian community activity. One such church in Leeds has cut the worshipping area of a former 3,000-pew seating building down to around 300. The rest of the church serves as an industrial training and community centre where local young people receive commercial, industrial and catering training and where at the same time they are given the experience of seeing the church in action. Generous government grants are available for such schemes.

No one who visits such establishments can fail to appreciate the satisfaction enjoyed by all who participate in this form of modern mission.

'Living with the poor' – *actually living* – can be done if the need is grasped and if church resources are sufficiently harnessed. Canon Sebastian Charles, long a critic of the *status quo*, is in no doubt of the need for action:

> Given the potential strength of the churches, the church must recruit men and women of the highest calibre and give them a sense of purpose and initiative to live in inner city areas and stay there.[12]

There is strength, too, in the suggestion that all clergy should be encouraged to spend a period of three to five years in an inner city parish, with the possibility of community work training. It would stand them in good stead in relating to their fellow clergy, their congregations and the people who live in the neighbourhood.

It will not be easy for the church to break the limitations of long-established structures which dictate much of resource allocation strategy. But the transformation must be made if urban mission is to have real meaning.

However, for all its failing, the church in the inner city commands considerable assets. It may be a minority but it is a serving minority and just 'being on the spot' does provide contact with people and produces a measure of credibility. 'Listening posts' are thus established for the wider congregation.

The church is also symbolized in the living presence of its members. In many deprived areas the only professional people left in the district at night are the local priest and ministers and their families. This living presence is an indispensable witness and is a sign language that the local residents easily understand and appreciate. Those who live within the problem have an authority to speak about that problem which the commuter cannot easily command.

A church presence can also do something to provide the sense of continuity and longer-term commitment which at local and national levels government so often fails to provide. This failure does much to destroy the confidence of those who live in the inner city. Joan Higgins, in a comment on her experiences in the early days of the urban programme, provides a devasting example of the failure of the Civil Service to build up relevant expertise: in the first five years of its existence, she calculates, the project survived three changes of government (with consequent changes of Home Secretary), at least four Under Secretaries and three Principals.[13]

The church building itself is potential common ground for all and nowadays the 'plant' of the church is used increasingly for community purposes far beyond the traditional purposes envisaged by an earlier congregation. Already in a host of nationwide employment action schemes a fellowship with the needy is being established which gives new meaning to urban mission.

In such a ministry to the poor the risks are great, but in the participation process we become involved in one of today's great human themes. The 1980 Melbourne Conference of the World Council of Churches provided a powerful new focus on the challenge of poverty. The occasion became for many a time of conversion. One English observer put it like this:

I was convinced by the repeated arguments from many different

> speakers that in the experience of the poor there is a vital entry into knowledge of God's Kingdom.[14]

Just as Christians in general in the West are beginning to appreciate through 'Partners in Mission' projects how much the churches of the Third World have to teach through interchange, so in our domestic situation, by putting itself at the service of the poorest, the church achieves a state of mission 'where Christ mysteriously awaits it, among those who are most down-trodden. We discover that 'the hidden presence of the Judge of the World in the least of our brethren is a judgment that tests the authenticity of the church and its mission'.[15]

To turn again to Bishop David Sheppard as he explains this special grace from a national perspective:

> If we can put ourselves in the shoes of the poor and disadvantaged, we may see how matters appear to their consciousness – not just inner city matters, but matters which affect the whole of our society.
>
> These are not side issues for some to pursue on the margins of the life of Christ and society. Nor are they the result of a political preference. They are to do with the righteousness of God which has a tendency to topple over in favour of those at a disadvantage.
>
> They are to do with God taking flesh in the person of Jesus, living out His life in a special relationship to the poor.[16]

In that special relationship the unemployment stamp of UB40 can carry no stigma. Instead, there must be fellowship if we are to make the transition to the new industrial order which beckons. The danger in the present (and likely to continue) situation of high unemployment is that tensions will build up causing us to fragment as a nation. The signs are everywhere that the so called protestant work ethic which has been for many the driving and binding force for more than two hundred years of industrial capitalism has run its course and in so doing is producing a battery of fundamental social problems searching for expression in new work relationships. We require a new moral drive which will keep us together during the watershed period. New ways of organizing industrial society, ways which are humane as well as profitable, must be sought. This will require a recognition of our national interdependence expressed corporately through the ways in which we organize our social and economic institutions.

For such a social revolution a national consensus must be sought and the church has a prime role to play in the seeking. The famine story of Genesis hints at what is needed. The children of Jacob, when they sought help from Joseph, were assured that all would be well if they returned to Egypt with their brother; but they were warned: 'Unless your youngest brother comes down with you, you shall see my face no more.'

For our generation there is a similar challenge. There is, indeed, corn in plenty for all – but only if we seek it in the company of our brother. In becoming truly ecumenical we become truly human – we are released to make the great transition with a confidence that is well founded.

6

A PRACTICAL RESPONSE TO THE WORK CRISIS

> 'Unemployment affects every aspect of life, from the material and physical to the mental and spiritual. It therefore very much concerns the church' (Pope John Paul II, Liverpool 1982).
>
> 'Now that one in seven British workers is unemployed it is even clearer than ever before that the Christian church in this country ought to be praying, thinking and caring to the utmost of its power. Here is a human tragedy which calls for the greatest sensitivity of pastors, social workers, parents, neighbours and fellow citizens – a sensitivity which can be inspired by the Lord whose eyes of compassion saw the men idle in the market place' (*Church Times*, 3.9.82).

One of the least publicized, but practical, inter-church caring programmes in recent years has been the Church Action with the Unemployed (CAWTU) Campaign, launched in February 1982 in the belief that caring members of the Christian churches can help to tackle the problems of unemployment. It is promoted by a group of people from the major Christian churches in Britain who are concerned about unemployment and social responsibility; chaired by Canon Frank Scuffham, industrial chaplain in Corby, it has been paid for by grants from the central funds of the supporting churches and from charitable trusts, with additional help from the Manpower Services Commission. Much of the work involved in mailing has been sponsored through the Community Enterprise Programme.

An 'Action Leaflet' went out to 25,000 clergy and lay people throughout the country asking local churches to mobilize their resources. Three main activities were listed:

1. *Pastoral Care* (to help people cope with being out of work):

'Drop-in' centres were suggested. Based on church premises, such centres would offer information, leisure and recreational facilities, and the promotion of congregational discussion on the changing role of work in life.

2. *Work Experience* (a better chance to get jobs): here the churches were encouraged to set up training workshops or to sponsor a scheme under the Manpower Services Commission and to provide adults who have been out of work for long periods with project opportunities of community benefit.

3. *Job Creation* (new jobs and permanent work): here the encouragement was to join with others in creating a new job, perhaps as a local church administrator or a maintenance officer. Neighbourhood co-operatives to develop local services and small industries were also advocated, as were industrial common ownership enterprises in which redundancy money might be used as start-up capital. Local employers would also be approached to expand their labour force.

What has been impressive about this campaign has been its practical nature. It has concentrated on local needs and has been based on the efforts of local people – it has challenged the alienation which so often accompanies unemployment. As the Revd Paul Brett, a national committee member has put it, he wanted to see 'a church working in partnership with other community groups to get things done'.

In a series of rethink proposals churches are reminded in the CAWTU leaflet that it will not be enough to create local jobs in the hope that things will pick up. The realism is stark, but stimulating:

> There is a growing conviction in Britain and elsewhere that the situation is changing rapidly and maybe permanently. When the economy picks up after the present recession there may still be several million 16 to 65-year-olds unable to find paid employment in the way it has been in the past. Serious thinking needs to be done about the nature of our society and the structure of our economy.[1]

All associated with the campaign, while conscious of the need for first-aid, are equally aware that deep down in the present economic crisis lie issues about the place and nature of work in society which must be debated and resolved. But until the bigger questions are resolved we must get on with doing what we can, where we can, and when we can to provide a local response. In so doing we will help locally and at the same time improve by our practical initiatives our contribution to the national debate. From my own experience of meeting people at the 'sharp end' of the problem I offer as guidelines for debate and practical action about the future of work:

1. Get from your church a commitment to the CAWTU campaign. 200,000 leaflets have been circulated – has your church returned the action reply slip?

2. Discover the facts in your area and promote debate on the local and national underlying issues.

3. Study the vocabulary of the work ethic and distinguish between terms like 'paid employment' and 'work' – or 'retirement' and 'redeployment'. In particular, do not equate unemployment with lack of work. There may not be many *paid* jobs on offer, but look around you and you will discover plenty of work that needs to be done. Improvements in the social services, better educational facilities, opportunities for leisure activities, environmental amenities – press for action in your area on such concerns.

4. Keep in contact with your local leaders of industry and commerce. And do not neglect the local government and parliamentary representatives – they may not know all the answers but they should be given the opportunity to hear the questions. For example, the diocese of Bristol recently asked Norman Tebbitt, Secretary of State for Employment, what the church could do to help solve his daily problems. Mr Tebbitt was delighted with the approach for, as he put it, he is used to people 'pouring more fuel on the fire'. Writing in the Bristol diocesan newsletter, *Three Crowns*, Mr Tebbitt had this to say:

> The partnership between government employment programmes on the one hand and local church assistance on the other can be very powerful. You are in an ideal position to locate those in need and those who can help within your diocese and parishes. You can bring them together, put them in touch with the appropriate government programme, and thereby give them a new lease of hope and life.

5. Trade union contact is also important. Many of your congregation will be members of unions. They are a very useful source of contact with local industry and through branch and trade council membership can keep the church in touch with a wide range of

interests and people. Invite your local trade union leaders to join your consultations and to help sponsor your projects. Rotary and Round Table offer comparable openings to the business community.

6. Examine the possibility of extending job opportunities. Are work-sharing or job-splitting practical propositions in your area? Some jobs are more suited than others to the process – do some research into local possibilities, especially where apprenticeships are concerned.

7. Job creation is another area to probe. The Manpower Services Commission (MSC) offers generous grants – what we are short of are ideas. But as experience in all parts of the country shows, work in abundance awaits the supply of labour and capital. Contact others who have experience. Also press your local public institutions to show a good example where job creation is concerned.

8. Lead by example – in other words let your church or community action group demonstrate the practicality of job creation. Even the creation of one job per church or extra jobs in social administrative centres will help. For example, most churches could do with full-time staff in addition to the minister – and the government will give a grant in aid.

9. How far should the church itself become labour intensive? The example set is not always good. Why, when population is so much greater than in the past, is there so often a *reduction* in the number of full-time workers – all in the name of labour-saving efficiency! The church is at fault here – economic and not spiritual considerations are to the fore. Church services are virtually non-existent in some of the most needy areas.

10. For more and more people retirement is becoming an issue ever earlier in life. Certainly we can no longer think of 'retirement' as being given nothing to do. What then do we really mean by the word? For active people, the cessation of their 'youth-to-maturity job', provided it carries an adequate pension, may mean the opening up of new opportunities. Indeed increasingly it must, if 'retirement' is to acquire 'reward meaning'; 'redeployment' becomes an issue.

11. How far does worship take note of the economic crisis? And is it done with sensitivity so as not to embarrass those who may not want to be 'marked out' as 'problem' people in the congregation? Prayers of course are helpful, but they must be generalized enough to allow all to join in as equals.

12. Have you appointed a work liaison officer in your congrega-

tion, someone who will act as a letter-box and a listening-post? And who will keep in touch with other local groups and national agencies? Such a man or woman can also build up the information research centre; indeed, this post might qualify under a job creation scheme.

So far over 200,000 leaflets giving practical advice on unemployment action schemes have gone out from the Birmingham Campaign headquarters and a special catalogue of employment projects lists 27 regional areas in Britain where work is underway. A countrywide network of contact people – 'brokers' – has been established through which enquirers can be put in contact with those who are actively involved. A list of some 50 'brokers' is available to those who return the answer slip which accompanies the action leaflet. The result has been encouraging. The 'drop-in' facility has been the most readily turned-to activity, but as confidence grows, and particularly as groups become aware of the range and amount of aid available, so too does the list of enterprises which provide new work. The following are practical examples of what is going on throughout the country:

On Merseyside, three Church of England parishes have grouped together to convert part of their church into a centre for the unemployed, offering counselling, a library, newspaper and light refreshments. It is a base for an MSC scheme organizing community projects in support of the elderly in the area. I have visited similar successful centres in North Wales and Yorkshire.

On Teesside the churches are involved in sponsoring 'care teams', each with a supervisor supporting six or eight unemployed school-leavers. The teams are funded through the MSC Youth Opportunities Programme and their work includes gardening and decorating for the elderly and helping to care for the children.

In Belfast a Rural Deanery of the Church of Ireland has established an association to repair and renovate local houses. With the support of a government grant, employment is provided for six local craftsmen in painting and decorating, joinery and general maintenance. A manager and typist are also employed. Ten per cent of the cost is met by the local churches and the services are offered on an ecumenical basis. Another local group of 400 church people have combined under united church leadership to buy shares to establish a small supermarket and post office in a neglected area. A free goods and newspaper delivery service for pensioners and the disabled is provided, as is also the collection and delivery of medical prescriptions.

From Manchester there is news that churches of all the denominations in Hulme and Moss Side have united in a jobs creation campaign. The scheme, funded by the MSC, aims to employ four people to be job creators for others, and the posts are being advertised at local Job Centres. It is expected that the team leader will be someone with managerial skills and initiative and that others in the team will offer social and community skills and interests. Meanwhile, at Stockton-on-Tees, Cleveland, 'Christian Relay', which seeks to utilize the skills of the early retired, has now recruited two full-time staff members, an administrator and assistant, with the support of the MSC.

In hard hit South Wales, when a major redundancy was impending at the local steel works, the Newport and Gwent industrial mission joined with other groups to pool skills and information. They set up a network giving details of all available counsellors and the skills they could offer. Network members combine their talents in the search for jobs and the provision of information.

In Scotland, the Iona Community and other Christian groups have long been in the front-line of the unemployment struggle. The problem is especially pressing among young people and many parishes make special provision for this group.

Less well publicized, but no less effective, in many parts of the country individual churches and church-linked organizations are adapting government schemes to their own particular needs. The Youth Opportunities Programme has been used to give many young people their first-job experience, often as a clerical assistant in the parish or manse office. Some parishes have benefited greatly by the employment of maintenance officers who keep the 'plant' in order. As one rural vicar wrote: 'It's amazing, I never thought that the MSC could provide me with such assistance – it's the best thing that's happened to the parish in years.' God works in wondrous ways. . .

The employment officers of the MSC are generally sympathetic to schemes which are well prepared and which meet an evident need. The definition of 'need' is generously interpreted and realistically assessed. Work on church records, correspondence and administrative back-up for minister and committees is held to 'count'; other examples include the appointment of an ecumenical training officer, a secretary shared by the Fellowship of Reconciliation and a local community group, and a churches' schools liaison officer.

Finally, a church-based activity of a more general nature: the Bishop of Ripon had the original idea of sponsoring a 'job creation ideas' competition. He got replies from all over the country, from people of all ages and from employed and unemployed. The £100 prize went to the plan for a regional waste exchange, to feed one industry with the waste thrown off by another.

It was a symbolic suggestion; a reminder that good returns can be obtained from the least expected sources. But the lesson is clear: we must be prepared to confront the problem and seek a solution, each in our own particular situation. When that is done we will find ourselves ready to join with others engaged in like activities.

The Church Action with the Unemployed Campaign will not of itself provide the answer to our social and economic problems, but it is a splendid and practical example of the local church in action, standing by its people when they are most in need. They are lighting candles, instead of cursing the darkness.

7

TRANSCENDING THE WORK ETHIC

> 'I know I shouldn't feel guilty at being unemployed because it's not my fault, but I do. I suppose it's something to do with the way we were brought up' (Student teacher, London).

We live in a time when what is called the 'work ethic', or sometimes the 'protestant work ethic', is a subject for public debate. Television, radio and the press are giving the topic the treatment. 'Why do we work', 'Does personal fulfilment depend on a job which provides money', 'Is there a difference between employment and work' – these and other questions are being asked at a world level with increasing urgency.

Such discussions about work are not new; utopian writers from sixteenth-century Thomas More have kept the topic to the fore. But never before in history have so many asked the same questions at the same time and on such an international scale.

As we have noted earlier, the work ethic has been on the intellectual agenda for a long time. Even the 'in' themes of today have been well rehearsed. 'Future Shock', 'The Third Wave' and such phrases derive from thinkers who did pioneering work early in this century. In particular, we stand on the shoulders of Lewis Mumford who in a series of memorable books alerted us to the vital links between industrial technology and patterns of civilization. In a new language to assist our perception of the problems we were urged to challenge the 'tempo of wage work life', to escape from our 'time cage', to seek 'the creative pause', to achieve 'dynamic equalibrium' and to build a 'life economy'. Above all, in an invitation which still stands, we were offered a new purpose for our lives:

> The function of work is to provide man with a living: not for the

> purpose of enlarging his capacities to consume but of liberating his capacities to create. The social meaning of work derives from the acts of creation it makes possible.[1]

Prime examples of Kenneth Clark's observation: 'The first flash of insight which persuades human beings to change their basic assumptions is usually contained in a few phrases.'[2]

Of special importance for an age which is reconsidering the work ethic is Mumford's recognition of the subtle interplay between work and leisure and the need to explore a better balance:

> Man's capacity to impose work on himself not merely gave him greater security and freedom but made possible a more highly organized kind of society. . . But in origin work and play have the same common trunk and cannot be detached: every mastery of the economic conditions of life lightens the burdens of servile work and opens up new possibilities for art and play; and in these realms man gains a fuller insight into his surroundings, his community, and himself. Thus man's released activities grow out of his conditioned activities: the esthetic flower out of the economic leaf.

And in a neat comment on a circle that must be squared:

> Without compulsory labour, civilizations would not originally have produced enough spare energy to maintain their higher activities. Without freedom from compulsory labour, man cannot enjoy these higher activities.[3]

But neither Mumford nor a host of distinguished disciples have been able to calm the fears of the multitudes who are caught up in the wage-work process. The apprehensions of the London teacher whose comment headed this chapter are widespread: 'I shouldn't feel guilty but I do. I suppose it's something to do with the way we were brought up.'

'The way we were brought up' – those few words take us to the heart of the work ethic difficulty. We are part of a generation, and descendants of generations, conditioned to regard wage-work as natural and necessary for human dignity – non-work pursuits are exceptions to the rule that man is a part of the productive process. Those who by lack of ability, infirmity or other mishap are unable to fit into this framework are deemed not to be 'industrious' and run the risk of being given a social exclusion order by society.

We may be over-neat about our definitions and may run the risk of careless generalization about mass attitudes, but equally those who are practical social engineers must take note of what are widely-held views about work, summed up under the description 'protestant work ethic'. Today's heirs to that tradition do not easily shake off their inheritance.

A recent discussion with a group of transport workers produced these views about what they felt the work ethic to be:

> It's in the Bible – 'in the sweat of thy face shalt thou eat bread'; and doesn't it say that 'Hard work is the lot of every man.'

> You know what you are through your job – when the job goes you lose part of yourself. You feel cast off.

> I've worked hard all my life and always earned my keep. I know I've paid for my insurance but I don't like getting money for doing nothing. That's what's depressing about social security. Those who tell you that you're only getting your rights have never had the experience.

> Leisure is all right, but a grown man cannot play around all day. You've got to earn your leisure with an honest day's work. I don't want to depend on anyone else to keep my family. If you don't work you don't eat – it's as simple as that.

> I was always taught at home and in school and chapel to have respect for the time that God gives us on earth. I see nothing wrong in using that time in honest work – there will always be time left over for leisure. The trouble with unemployment is that it's all leisure and no work.

And finally a perceptive remark from the oldest in the group (a man in his sixties) who admitted his unsureness:

> It's not easy to change a lifetime's ways. I once worked down the mines. It was a real hell-hole and I was glad to escape. Yet it's sad to see the way in which men feel they have to struggle to keep some of those torture chambers open. There must be more to work than that. In a really civilized society we would be getting as many people as possible out of dangerous jobs and giving them

> something more pleasant to do. But I don't think you are going to change ideas about work quickly – you are going to have to re-educate a whole generation and see that our youngsters are better taught to know what to do with spare time.

The ghosts of Luther, Calvin, Adam Smith and Samuel Smiles arise among those remarks. Morals and economics are firmly linked. The job admits one to the high tables of the economic system where goods are made. Money tokens are received by those who labour, so ensuring a place at the consumer counter. For those who cannot earn tokens special provision has to be considered.

There is also a strong suggestion that leisure and work are things apart. 'Time' is special and precious; it is dedicated to production and must not be 'wasted' – left-over hours (spare time) are contributed to home and family. Making a living and *living* have become separate undertakings.

Sadly – and most difficult to overcome in a society with limited educational and leisure rights facilities – there is the clear identification of personal value with what one 'earns-at' and the conviction that we are diminished gravely by job loss. The firmly held equation of work with job is underlined in every comment – 'real' work is what we do for wages in a factory situation. Perhaps, tenable enough as an attitude when there are jobs sufficient to ensure the link between production and consumption – but socially devastating in its contradictions if we live in a society where productivity is high and labour demand low.

Our final contribution got nearest to the dilemma of the time: 'There must be more to work than that.' And so there must, if work is to become more than a crutch. We are back to an earlier question: if, as seems likely, a progressive reduction of labour is inevitable, do we begin to provide for occupation without work and do we learn to develop needs and find ways to meet those needs which go beyond the confines of what we know as the modern economy? Can we replace an industrial culture that has run its course?

The views of these working men – and they are widely held – illustrate the way in which the spirit of capitalism has seeped into industrial society, made all the more powerful in its grip, as some of the comments hint, by echoes of the religious justification provided by Luther and Calvin and their theological successors.

Writing in *The Secular City* nearly twenty years ago, Harvey Cox made the point in a wider context:

> In the Western World, human work presents a striking example of how we allow residual religious meanings to cling to an activity long after its authentic function has been secularized. We prove this by equating work with a job, a paid position supplied by the market. . . Our confusion of human work with a job produced by the market economy proves that our attitudes towards work have not yet been liberated from religious or metaphysical meanings, often held below the level of consciousness. We have in technopolis the technical and social basis for the emancipation of work. We could transform it from a drudgery into a delight. Yet we still cling to pious attitudes about work, predispositions inherited from a different era. But we shall have to lay aside this idol too. Technopilis demands a new definition of work.'[4]

Though the theological framework has been weakened the grip is still strong enough to do damage. Indeed, as a recent Methodist study suggests, the status of today's unemployed is greatly diminished by prevailing social attitudes which imply that those who do not work (i.e. receive wages or have private wealth) are different, marginalized, people. Because of the numbers involved in this conclusion, a special urgency enters into the search for new standards by which we may be valued in society. The 'two nation' situation is no longer approaching – it has arrived.[5]

In any debate about moral 'benchmarks' the church is well-placed to make a contribution, and as controversy over the Falklands and 'The Bomb' has shown, it is still in a position to claim substantial media attention on national issues. However, where the work ethic is concerned the church will find itself as having 'many a sin to answer for' – too often in industrial affairs early theologies of work reinforced the economic *status quo* and failed to provide a critical and emancipatory analysis.

Today's theologians of work are more aware of the link between structural changes affecting the condition of labour and social justice and are conscious of the part that work patterns play in human consciousness. Of equal importance, the church is being asked to explore the proposition that there may be no return to full employment and hence we may require a spiritual outlook that enables people to remain humanly and psychologically at ease (difficult, as we have seen in a previous chapter) even if they do not work. So an even more profound question arises: 'Has the time come when the church must help society to transcend the work ethic?'

Unfortunately the church has come late in the day to a fuller appreciation of the importance of work in people's lives; and in a fast-changing industrial scene the catching up process is not easy. Indeed, many critics of the church are likely to respond, 'Is your interest really necessary?'[6]

But if the church is to be blamed for helping to thrust its people into a work ethic straightjacket it is only fair to record that the sin was often one of omission rather than commission. Certainly for the Christian Fathers 'work' was not a subject high on the theological agenda. It was not that the subject was regarded as being outside the scope of God's redeeming action; it was more that the matter was a taken-for-granted part of life. Unfortunately this complacency extended into and beyond the Industrial Revolution. As a pioneer British study in 1960 put it:

> 'Work' was simply not a problem, and therefore did not become a theological problem. It was not a subject which groups of Christians would have sat down to discuss for a week. Work as a problem, and therefore a theological problem, is something quite new. At the earliest we could not have become self-conscious about work until well into the Industrial Revolution. The novelty of the methods of work, the exigencies of mass production, the social consequences and, finally, the church's so-called loss of the working class – all these combine to make 'work' into a problem.[7]

Nor does the Bible provide a ready guide. Though the Old Testament is vastly more informed on work relationships than the Gospels, it is not easy to base a modern theology of work on what is recorded in a good deal of what one scholar has called 'inconclusive fragmentariness'.

But it is not only the church which has been at fault in showing interest. Much nearer our own time, E. F. Schumacher underlined the neglect which all disciplines have accorded the subject:

> Considering the centrality of work in human life one might have expected that every text book on economics, sociology, politics and related subjects would present a theory of work as one of the indispensable foundation stones for all future expositions. After

> all it is work which occupies most of the energies of the human race and what people actually *do* is normally more important for understanding them, than what they say, or what they spend their money on, or what they own, or how they vote. However, the truth of the matter is that we look in vain for any presentations of theories of work in these textbooks. The question of what the work does to the worker is hardly ever asked, not to mention the question of whether the real task might not be to adapt the work to the needs of the worker rather than to demand that the worker adapt himself to the needs of the work – which means, of course, primarily to the needs of the machine.[8]

Perhaps, after all, it is better to agree with one of the conclusions of John M. Todd's influential Downside Inquiry into Christian thought and practice:

> It may be suggested that we will not find a satisfactory Christian theology of work ready-made for us in the past, and that the twentieth century has to work out its own situations in the light of twentieth century conditions, even though what men have thought about work in the past may help us in some degree to avoid their errors and profit from their wisdom.[9]

Writing about a much earlier period, R. H. Tawney stressed that even the mediaeval attitude to work was difficult to define. Certainly it was no golden age for the masses. Far from being a band of happy producers working in idyllic conditions, the masses were more likely to be at the mercy of the elements, famine and authoritarian rule. The Revolt of 1381, the protests of John Ball and the poetry of Langland remind us of a mediaeval society that was far from ideal for the peasantry.

Nor can we be sure that those who did express opinions about manual labour represented the views of those who actually performed the labour. Most of the latter were illiterate and were unlikely to have philosophized much about their working conditions. When working people begin to record their impressions it is clear that they were not over influenced by 'calling' theories emanating from the church. More typical of their down-to-earth attitudes were the jingles (still part of working-class folklore):

You will eat by and by
In the glorious land above the sky.
Work and pray, live on hay,
You'll get pie in the sky
When you die (it's a lie)!

or equally cynical, this Great Depression verse:

And why don't you work like other folk do?
How the hell can I work when there's no work to do?

Hallelujah, I'm a bum,
Hallelujah, bum again.
Hallelujah give us a hand out,
To revive us again.

But impressed or not by uplifting lectures on the dignity of labour, the working classes were greatly influenced by a powerful church-based intellectual lobby which provided justification for the aims and practices of the proponents of the eighteenth-century Industrial Revolution. This defence of the system was the continuation of a process of endorsement given to new patterns of economic life between the sixteenth century and later periods.

The change in the attitude of church and society towards the economic order – 'the reversal of the thinkable' – has been neatly summarized:

> The reversal of attitudes towards the economic sphere in the Christian West can be discerned, particularly, through the evolution of the definition of the poor. In the Middle Ages, the poor man was honoured as the symbol of Jesus Christ, who was to be welcomed with open-handed hospitality. This concept was later replaced by one in which the poor man was considered as a lazy vagabond who had to be locked up in order to be taught the meaning of work and discipline.[10]

The writings of Luther and particularly Calvin gave a powerful thrust to the change in attitude producing what Max Weber later called 'the spirit of capitalism' – a protestant work ethic making theologically respectable the drive to make money and to create a social and economic system built on competitive relationships.

Not all churchmen accepted the conventional economic wisdom of *laissez-faire*, but they were in a minority and were castigated for breaking rank. However in the closing decades of the twentieth century their ideas are returning with renewed vigour. John Ruskin proved one of the most effective critics of the theory of competition and its effect on society. As he summed it up in a famous aphorism which has lost none of its force:

> Government and co-operation are in all things and eternally the laws of life. Anarchy and competition eternally and in all things, the laws of death.[11]

This was too much for the Establishment. Gentle John Ruskin was regarded as a heretic threatening Victorian society. The voice of the Manchester merchant was heard in *The Times*:

> If we do not crush him, his wild words will touch the springs of action in some hearts, and before we are aware, a moral floodgate may fly open and drown us all.[12]

Ruskin, and with him, William Morris, did much to keep alive visions of an earlier and a future vision of work, less profit-seeking, more fulfilling. Ruskin in particular in his rounded view of labour is helpful as in our own day we make a reassessment:

> God intends every man to be happy in his work. It is written, 'in the sweat of they brow,' but it was never written, 'in the breaking of thine heart,' thou shalt eat bread . . . Now in order that people may be happy in their work, these three things are needed: they must be fit for it; they must not do too much of it; and they must have a sense of success in it – not a doubtful sense, such as needs some testimony of other people for its confirmation, but a sure sense, or rather knowledge, that so much work has been done well, and fruitfully done, whatever the world may say or think about it. So that in order that a man may be happy, it is necessary that he should not only be capable of his work, but a good judge of his work.'[13]

But in the England of Ruskin's day the formers of public opinion and the church in general were more responsive to views like Carlyle's 'perennial nobleness and even sacredness in work' and Samuel Smiles' 'humble profound and most religious consciousness that work is the appointed calling of men on earth'. Such luminaries represented an industrial revolution that had yet to run its course.

The rebuff to Ruskin was to be expected. As his biographer comments:

> We must realize that in 1860, orthodox political economy was the theology of the only effective nineteenth-century religion. Its complex, abstract and at times impenetrable arguments, gave to the middle-class heirs of the Industrial Revolution the feeling of certainty and mystic protection which scholastic philosophy had provided in the Middle Ages.[14]

Today much of that certainty has vanished as industrial society finds itself in what one philosopher has called 'a sea with no maps'.

But two hundred years ago it was different. The Industrial Revolution has put the protestant work ethic firmly on its throne – hard work and heaven, too! What in former times had been a way of life to be questioned against eternal standards became the new norm, sanctified by the church. R. H. Tawney in a magnificent flourish put it well:

> Baptized in the bracing, if icy, waters of Calvinist theology, the business of life, once regarded as perilous to the soul, acquired a new sanctity. Labour is not merely an economic means; it is a spiritual end.
>
> The idea of economic progress as an end to be consciously sought, while ever receding, had been unfamiliar to most earlier generations of Englishmen, in which the theme of moralists had been the danger of unbridled cupidity, and the main aim of public policy had been the stability of traditionalists. It found a new sanction in the identification of labour and enterprise with the service of God.[15]

The identification of labour and enterprise with some sort of higher service remains with us – less God-centred, but still associated with notions of 'good behaviour'. Our major political, industrial and cultural institutions are permeated with the work ethic – party leaderships preach the message; unions and management display solidarity on the issue; and schools throughout the land prepare our young people for a world which will not be there when they seek to enter it. Again, our hopes for the future rest on a battery of assumptions whose base is manifestly being eroded.

But though there are many (particularly those in secure employment) who tell their threatened neighbours to 'keep calm', this advice is being increasingly discounted as men and women on any international scale begin to challenge what one utopian has called

'The Last Age of Confusion'. By the lives they are leading these messengers of change begin to question the concept of man as a mere money-maker, as a cog in the competitive system, or as an adjunct of new technology. We are learning again that people in community act long before institutionalized theories take note of the need for adaptation. In such situations the *status quo* is confronted with a 'hunch' alternative reflecting a new appreciation of real world facts of life.

The 'new look' is none the less real for being vaguely formulated. Christopher Bryant's suggestion that 'It is not so much a commonly held set of opinions, as a change of spectacles through which people perceive the world of work and leisure, of family and society and politics,' is helpful. Below the level of consciousness there is a stirring of alternatives which comes to the surface long before they are capable of conceptualization.

The offering of 'alternatives' is now proceeding, as pressures to transform the work ethic build-up. Many of these pressures are external to our own country – in particular, demands from the Third World for parity of esteem reflected in the Brandt Report and other North-South studies. Three areas of dogma behind the work ethic are particularly under attack: the glorification of the individual, the suggestion that the chief end of man is work, and the competitive base for economic activity.

Interestingly, and encouragingly, as disenchantment with the existing *status quo* spreads, the campaign for revision brings together a political cross-section. So Conservative Edward Heath joins with Socialist Willy Brandt in calling for a new world economic order. In our own country there is increasingly behind the scenes an informal agenda of concern which links management and labour and party-political activists.

A recent book by former Labour MPs Ivor Clemitson and George Rodgers illustrates the point from the 'left'. In a courageous argument for a replacement of the work ethic the writers challenge the traditional attitudes of their own Party and call on the trade unions to move beyond their out-of-date confines. A powerful case is made out for an economic analysis of unemployment which takes into account a questioning of the work ethic and a consequential questioning of many 'sacred cows' on either side of the political divide:

If the work ethic is not challenged then, inevitably, we are left

> with only two possible alternatives – full employment and unemployment – and we are prevented from seeing new perspectives and devising new policies based upon those new perspectives. . . What we are seeking to do is to argue that there are far sounder bases for socialist argument than a narrowly conceived work ethic; bases which are far more appropriate to the age into which we are moving. In short, we need to develop a 'life ethic' rather than a 'work ethic' and the corresponding concept of 'full life' rather than 'full employment'.[16]

It is also interesting to note that, far from being 'drummed out' for their views, Clemitson and Rodgers have received endorsement in a foreword by influential Party spokesman Neil Kinnock, who writes:

> The work ethic, so long dominant in Western society, is the main target of their attack, and they present the cogent view that it must be replaced by a broader, deeper ethic concerned with the fullness and wholeness of life and which has to become the primary goal of political policy. Their idea is not an alibi for laziness or a lotus-eater's manifesto. It is a tangible alternative to the nightmare future of mass unemployment and social uproar, and subservience to technological change. The simple alternative between employment and unemployment must be transcended by policies which are designed to provide creative and positive non-work alternatives to both employment and unemployment.[17]

An imaginative host to fortune should ever Mr Kinnock become Leader of his Party.

Much of this ferment is a tribute to the growing reality of interdependence at national and international levels. What is needed now is an application of the principle in our national life through a re-examination of the work ethic and the economic system on which it is dependent.

Application of the principle will require a change of attitude on the part of some of our strongest institutions. If, for instance, we are to avoid a 'two-nation' situation, is it possible to continue the free bargaining system for wages which both employees and unions favour? To the strongest the spoils?

And if the wage-work system cannot guarantee a just distribution of wealth, can those who are in possession of the jobs continue to enjoy a monopoly position? Does sharing stop at the factory gate? Equally, if a new 'mix' between work and leisure is to be achieved, how far can the institutions of society be persuaded to change their rules to facilitate the process? Job sharing alone would be a major contribution, requiring considerable institutional flexibility.

And, of fundamental importance, how do we ensure a redistribution of wealth in society sufficient to make possible the fuller-life-for-all implicit in the notion of an interdependent nation? Without such a redistribution, 'sharing one another's burdens' will have a hollow ring about it.

In any reassessment of the role of work in society the educationists will be called upon to play a key part. Can we then achieve a curriculum for our times, not only to do with the 'nuts and bolts' of education but with the values we inculcate? In particular, we require a curriculum which will encourage our children, as they grow up in 'the global village', to replace the opium of competition with a dynamic which is corporate in scope and centred on co-operation.

H. G. Wells, in his *Men Like Gods*, looked to such an educated society as the only hope for mankind. He recognized that the legalized struggle of men and women to get the better of one another was based on primitive instincts too dangerous to endure. Only through new ideas and new conventions of human association could the human race avoid disaster and collapse.

For Wells, as for so many in our contemporary world, co-operation seemed the way forward:

> The idea of competition to possess, as the ruling idea of intercourse, is like some ill-controlled furnace, threatening to consume the machine it had formerly driven. The idea of creative service has to replace it. To that end the human mind and will has to be turned if social life is to be saved.[18]

Such matters are of central concern to the whole nation – yet our system of political confrontation is ill-suited to achieve the level of discussion (as distinct from partisan debate) required.

I have suggested elsewhere[19] the creation of a Ministry of Job Creation and Preservation with special responsibility for monitoring and considering the human consequences of technical innovation and for giving advice. Such a Ministry would provide a focus for public concern and would keep on the Parliamentary agenda concerns which if neglected will gravely divide the nation.

But if the nation is to be truly involved in the great debate about where we are going we need to go beyond the Parliamentary sphere. In this respect what is called for is a Standing Advisory Commission on Post-Industrial Society, with a brief to keep before the nation and government the changing shape of our society and the ways in which the nation is being affected by developments in social and industrial structure. Such a forum would be well placed to study and influence the critical balance between work and leisure and to monitor relevant developments overseas. The forum would also put at the disposal of the nation a considerable body of expertise which at present works largely on a free-lance basis.

In any case, and whatever the pace and action of government and other secular institutions, the church must be prepared to act as a responding community, helping the nation to achieve a sense of direction which will underline our oneness as a people as we shape (and are shaped by) the new social-industrial order which is emerging all around us.

In this respect we would do well to study and encourage the considerable body of men and women who in everyday life are seeking a stable future in the unsettled present. These are those whom we have already noted; the people with a 'hunch' alternative; those who believe that it *is* possible to build a better world, even with the doubtful odds which are offered. I call these men and women, Pathfinders: lovers of our planet, who feel a responsibility for God's creation and wish to give true meaning to the lives of all his people. The Pathfinders know that there is a place for work in our lives, but they know also that it is only part of what we are and what we can do.

Pathfinders represent a growing ground-swell of change in our society and in societies elsewhere. Often unaware of the revolution they represent, they get on with day-to-day experiments in living and work, from which a new 'way-of-looking-at-life' will flow; they confront modern technology with caution, but without fear, and they explore a tenable accommodation. They are well motivated. Once again we find that practical witness, powered by the spirit, is in advance of theory.

Our Pathfinders are the true messengers of change; it is to their myriad activities that we now turn.

8

PATHFINDERS: COPING WITH THE GREAT TRANSITION

> 'The transition is under way; there is no going back on it. We must learn to use its enormous potential for good rather than for evil. Either we must wander hopelessly in the world or we must press forward to Zion' (Kenneth E. Boulding).

In 1931 H. G. Wells was asked to predict a future for fifty years ahead. It proved a gloomy prediction. Fortunately for the world, we have avoided some of the greatest calamities, but at times it has been a close thing.

For Wells we were in a grim contest:

> Some years ago I wrote that the salvaging of civilization was a race between education and catastrophe. Nowadays I am forced to add a qualification. Catastrophe indeed travels briskly, but education has not even started.

However, there were still options:

> The way toward a great world state of power, freedom and general happiness is still plainly open to mankind. We have been brought to the very border of the Promised Land of Progress. There is no inevitability in the approaching catastrophe. I confess I see no signs whatever of any such awakening as might save us, but who can tell what might be happening among the young, among the intelligent and wilful, outside one's range? It would need nothing superhuman to avert the decline. We are not being beaten in an honourable struggle; we are loitering and rotting down to disaster. But given that wave of sanity, that sudden miraculous resolve to

> stop this foolery today, and what sort of world might we not have before another half-century has passed?[1]

Wells' faith in the young is well placed – they are prominent in the ranks of the Pathfinders on which our hopes for making the great transition must rest. Given the opportunity, our children will learn to swim with the new tide and begin to direct its flow.

There are still vast numbers of young people who are denied anything like their place in the technological sun, but alongside this neglect there is also a growing consciousness of the need to involve the younger generation in preparations for a new industrial order. Indeed we have little option, because the young, more than any generation, are at ease with the 'mysteries' of the new technology. The saying has it: 'If you want to know the way to a computer ask a child.'

Information Technology Year 1982 made us more aware of the point. As exhibitions up and down the country showed, young children and students adapt easily to computer innovation; the pocket calculators and the speed with which they swept our classrooms in a few years had been important straws in the wind. Now the current government policy with its aim to ensure that all secondary schools have at least one computer – with, as a next step, computers in all 20,000 primary schools – is underway. ITY stressed that their object was not simply to get children interested in computers and familiar with them: they hoped to provide enormously powerful teaching aids which would help to develop imagination as well as learning.

Many educationists still point to negative features in the new situation, but there is a growing consensus that we have no alternative but to move with the times and to ensure that our educational system benefits from the gifts of science. Richard Fothergill, a leading figure in the 'Micro Electronics in Education Programme', warns us:

> The rapid growth of micro-technology in recent years is really quite frightening. The computers which we have now in our schools were not available some five years ago; the equipment which is new to us today will be out of date in a very short time. Education cannot afford to sit back and hope that technology will settle down. The bandwagon is running and we have to climb aboard quickly.[2]

Our youngest Pathfinders are climbing aboard the bandwagon in growing numbers. How they react when they get there will in large part determine the shape of the future. Fortunately they seem more at ease with what is going on than do their parents and grandparents. But as Einstein once remarked, 'imagination is more important than knowledge'. Our young people must be helped to receive and recognize new technology as a gift from God, to be used with care and compassion.

Their task is great. It is well summed up in a story emanating from America. A supermarket customer was in dispute with a girl operating an electronic check-out till. 'It must be right', said the girl. 'That machine is smarter than I am.'

The girl at the next counter turned to her fiercely and said, 'if you think that, you're dead.'[3]

Which of these was the true Pathfinder!

An older generation, though not as adept at dealing with the 'hardware' of new technology, welcomes the promised potential and looks to a release from much labour that has been burdensome. In particular, the union of science and technology makes possible the abolition of physical poverty and deprivation. U Thant, former Secretary-General of the United Nations, once invited us to grasp this opportunity:

> The central stupendous truth about developed economies today is that they can have the kind and scale of resources they decide to have. It is the decision that makes the resources. This is the fundamental revolutionary change – perhaps the most revolutionary we have ever known.[4]

In other words we are no longer constrained by production difficulties to provide for all God's children (yet 40,000 of them die each day from starvation); our limitations arise because we have not yet learned to match the needs of individuals to the supplies which are available. We have allowed ourselves to become trapped within an outmoded economic system and spending patterns (particularly on arms) which inevitably produce serious human needs. Our servant has become our master – we bow down to a graven image.

Roger Clarke, in a penetrating conclusion, has identified our predicament as something which goes much deeper than any party political matter – and he is right:

> For what I see in the present situation constitutes a fracture of fellowship, the recreation and perpetuation of an underclass in the midst of otherwise comparative affluence.[5]

If we have the vision to do so we can break out of that predicament. The counter attack must begin at the point of challenging the domination of our money work ethic by moving towards a society which has as its main thrust an ethic which is service and 'life' based. It will not be easy; we shall need a good deal of the 'optimism of grace' on which so many of the saints have depended; it is perhaps our greatest ecumenical challenge.

Bishop David Brown in his last great book said it all in a wider context:

> I believe that the End is in God's hands, and that it will completely transcend anything that we can imagine. It will be a human community marked by rich diversity and universal harmony: it will reach beyond space and time into eternity.

And as we face the immediate future we cannot better his last piece of practical advice:

> Meanwhile as we hope for tomorrow, there are today things for us all to do, to whatever faith we belong, in preparation for it.[6]

In our present day the old and the new ways mingle as they must, but it is clear that alternatives pointing to other ways of organizing social and industrial affairs are being offered by men and women who in an unconscious unison are discovering that there *is* another way of work and life, vastly different from that which has been the lot of previous generations. The Pathfinders have set in train a revolution, but for the most part it is not immediately recognized or acknowledged as such.

Working-class Pathfinders

In all great social upheavals the working class are most deeply involved; they may not write the books, but they work out the theory in practice. For many who are caught up in the present 'work' revolution, it has become a case of recognizing, for better or worse, that the old order is changing and that 'things will never be the same again'. This opinion is widely held and in some respects the industrial workers have shown more realism than any other group. (This realism should not be taken as resignation, and it is important that other groups in society respond positively to the change in attitude.)

'Signals' are being released. Joe Wade, General Secretary of the influential National Graphical Association is a case in point. He spoke to his Union conference in Eastbourne in 1982:

> I have to say to you that unless we are prepared to take on board the full implications of new technology, unless we are prepared to become more flexibile in our attitudes, and unless we are prepared to co-operate in improving productivity within the industry, we shall be engulfed by a tidal wave of technology which we will not be able to control. We cannot ignore the stark reality of the position which now confronts us because . . . if we are not prepared to embrace new technology in a manner which will transform the newspaper industry into a highly competitive one (unless we are prepared to face up to the need to improve efficiency and productivity throughout the whole of the industry) the competition from alternative sources and technology in this country or from abroad will spell the death knell of the industry as we have known it in the past.[7]

Joe Wade is only the more publicized of many union leaders who have decided to 'go along' with new technology – the wedding may have started off as 'shotgun', but it shows signs of working out.

Confirmation of this reluctant acceptance is contained in the 1982 Report of the Labour Research Department (an independent trade union financed research body). It is concluded that workers have a 'generally positive' attitude towards the introduction of micro-chip technology, even though it leads to job losses in one office in three. Management too, are seen as learning the value of new technology agreements. In most cases there is consultation before the technology is introduced and it is argued that the existence of so many agreements on this issue is evidence that the micro-chip is accepted as 'a matter for negotiation'. Such agreements open up the way for a considerable measure of social control.

It is also noticeable that trade unionists do not offer opposition on grounds of 'de-skilling'. More than half believe that new technology has brought increased responsibilities and opportunities for promotion.

The possibility of getting more free time through technology is also envisaged. A continuing demand from the TUC is for a 35-hour week, with longer holidays and early retirement schemes. Hours of work are falling below 40 per week and basic holidays continue to rise towards five weeks – all trends which open up a more flexible work-leisure relationship. However, a much more radical adjustment in working patterns will be required if work is to be more evenly spread – there is little uniformity in the present pattern and even less social justice.

There is a tendency for commerce and industry to over-rate the difficulty in changing patterns of working hours. Flexi-time was resisted for generations in this country until experience from abroad filtered through. Even the so-called economic burden of a shorter week needs close examination. The exact relationship between national output and working hours is by no means clear. Certainly it is unwise to assume that longer hours is the best way to higher production. For example, during Mr Heath's enforced 3-day week in 1970 national output did not fall by the expected 40%. Some calculations put the fall as low as 10%, with workers on the whole enjoying the new work style.

In fact, the distinction between compulsory work and compulsive work is being more widely acknowledged, especially by younger workers. When opposition to new machinery does arise it reflects not so much opposition to the machine as a demand for guarantees about the future of the operative. Such 'Luddism' has a creative aspect to it.

We should welcome the tendency of industrial people to be more 'choosy' about the work they are offered. Hopefully the day may arrive when workers will strike against unnecessary labour – and will question more firmly whether what they do is socially harmful. For example, the refusal to work on weapons of mass destruction has been so far a largely intellectual protest. What a different world it would be if the 'Bomb', if drugs, if pornography found themselves without human skills to give them meaning.

We need to recognize the essential pointlessness of much of modern wage work. Critics who are quick to term Manpower Services programmes as 'not real jobs' are strangely quiescent in the face of a modern avalanche of planned obsolescence and 'hidden persuader' created wants. Herman Daly asks in 'Towards a Steady-State Economy', 'Why do people produce junk and cajole other people into buying it? Not out of any innate love for junk or hatred of the environment, but simply in order to earn an income.' Daly rightly concludes that we need some principle of income distribution that is independent of the income-through-jobs link.[8]

Many able people live lives of quiet despair in their job situation and have no alternative; what an option to offer as an outlet for creative talents. Pointless labour is our greatest wastrel. To quote one professional worker: 'Most of us have jobs that are too small for our spirit.'

Earlier retirement – a more abundant life

Job dissatisfaction may be one of the reasons for the growing interest being taken in schemes of 'early retirement' increasingly sponsored and supported by both sides of industry. Often the driving force behind such schemes is the desire to create vacancies at the younger end of the labour force, rather than a desire to ensure a more satisfactory life and reward for those who have made their 'productivity' contribution to society. (Some societies see it differently: in one kibbutz I visited recently a worker of fifty-five told me that he had been given a lighter and less time-consuming job so that he could devote more of his mature experience to developing his personal interests and those of his local community.)

But whatever the reason, increasing advantage will certainly be taken of what we still call 'retirement' schemes. In a 1982 Report, funded by Guardian Royal Exchange, three-quarters of the people questioned said they would like to retire early and 54% were prepared to pay more taxes to boost their pensions. Only 4% of those who were asked about early retirement without loss of pension opted to continue working and 32% wanted to retire as soon as possible. Other investigations nationally and abroad confirm these trends. When the universities published an early retirement scheme the national headlines read 'Dons queue up for early redundancy' and when the French government in 1980 decided to promote early retirement it was presented with an embarrassing over-subscription of volunteers.

What *is* clear is that large numbers are willing to leave their major lifetime occupation so long as they can do so in dignity and reasonable comfort. The resistence to enforced retirement is real and natural when it may be the prelude to an end life (nowadays a considerable proportion of one's total existence) of economic hardship. For example, pensioners have to reduce their lifelong savings to £2,500 before they are entitled to supplementary benefit.

But behind the pressure for earlier job release is a factor of new and great sociological importance – the realization that one of the most remarkable achievements of the twentieth century has been the gift of ageing. Unlike previous generations we have it within our capacity to ensure the promise of a fuller and longer life. No more can we talk about a minority who sit in the corner resigned to decline. As a remarkable special edition of *New Internationalist* put it:

> Things are changing. In the last few years, the militancy of older citizens themselves, together with the exertions of some intelligent concerned people, have begun to make a dent in the monolith of ignorance and prejudice. More and more it is being realized that old people need what *people* need: personal autonomy and dignity, a useful role in society and appropriate affordable health care. Few Western governments can be unaware of the demographics of the future. And there are few politicians who do not hear the tramp of senior feet behind them.[9]

The conventional wisdom about age is being increasingly challenged: pensions are costly – but the introduction of pensions and every rise since has been resisted on 'cannot afford' slogans, notwithstanding the other 'affordables' enjoyed by a society based on the sacrifices of a previous generation; the old are accused of taking more out of society than they give, even when they are compulsorily retired; and they are told that they are 'over the top' even when it is 'performance', not age, that should count. For example, a considerable proportion of our state and private empires are run by men well into their energetic sixties or seventies – British Leyland, and the state enterprises of air, coal, transport, shipbuilding are only a few of many examples. The assumption that age equals decline is being and will be increasingly questioned as *choice* retirement for the masses becomes more possible.

For that reason it would be unwise to assume that the great and growing proportion of the population will be prepared to sit on the 'social shelf'. There is increasing evidence that once the threat of poverty can be discounted a positive response in terms of redeployment ambitions emerges:

> We get a move from tangible economic values to intangible social values; a change from individual to group values; a change from acquisition of goods to a seeking of fulfilment; a change from enjoyment of clear roles and functions, to a desire and hope for *new* clear roles and functions.[10]

Today's pensioners are no mere revamped versions of a generation that has gone before. They represent at their best a new life-force which sees 'retirement' not as an end but as a climax – a release to experiment; and to approach and grapple with things that really matter. There also are Pathfinders, joining in the dawn chorus of a new creation.

Our society – and particularly the political parties – must regard 'pensioners' as something more than 'move-over people', to be used as a scapegoat in an unemployment dilemma which is not of their making. A pension must denote that you have 'made it', not 'had it'.

Trade union influence

In the retirement issue, as in many others to do with the shaping of a new industrial order, trade unions can play a crucial role – but if they are to be fully effective they must be prepared to see themselves as more than a vehicle for the collective bargaining goals of their members. Jack Jones, for instance, before and after his retirement as General Secretary of the Transport and General Workers' Union, has been powerful in his advocacy of trade union support for those who have made 'a massive contribution' to the progress of the nation before retirement.

Unions in composition are almost unique among voluntary associations with a potentially massive outreach – numerically vast, inter-social, inter-racial, inter-generational and inter-regional. Something like a 'new model' unionism is called for to revalue the movement's potential and to ensure that the brotherhood and sisterhood, which at its best it represents, is put at the disposal of the whole community. The service ethic runs deep at the heart of unionism even though from time to time it is seriously eroded when it follows the selfish logic of the economic system inside which it operates.

Any call for a bias to the poor would be pretty pointless if unions did not play a part. On a matter like membership, for instance, much could be done to give the unemployed a feeling of 'belonging' by continuing union membership and the right to branch participation regardless of whether employed or not. It is surely an unexpected vagary that unions, of all bodies, should allow their membership roll to be decided by the ups and downs of the capitalist system.

Equally, as training schemes develop one looks to the day when every young person would be covered – either in 'normal paid employment' or by government training schemes. Here the challenge is to unions to establish parity of esteem between both work experiences – and to admit all apprentices, whether in the 'productive' sector or the training sector, to full union membership. Those in training should be given their professional 'card' – the only difference would be that they would be 'waiting for jobs'. Better surely to wait within the trade union family and to enjoy the fellowship and sense of identity afforded.

A 1983 initiative by Frank Chappell, President of the TUC and electricians' leader, shows sensitivity on this point. Alarmed by the decline in apprenticeship opportunities inside the industry, Mr Chappell and his colleagues have devised a new apprenticeship scheme which will enable apprenticeship to commence at any age and permit entrance to the trade to be achieved in large part by qualifications based on study and examinations rather than paid employment.

Hopefully, too, employers might make special provision for such young people 'in waiting' – visits to industrial premises, membership of works' clubs, involvement in special company functions. All such would do much to break down the divide which at present separates those with and those without a job. In some sectors like teaching, for example, the presence of 'teachers in waiting', as class-room assistants, would be a positive boon to over-worked full-timers and to those in search of in-service experience.

The problems to do with insurance benefits, union contributions and so on are formidable, but they pale in significance when viewed against present alternatives to those who are economic casualties. They suffer a double burden – no job and little fellowship. It is this latter combination which for many constitutes the real difference which accompanied unemployment – it is one of our most damaging 'differences', difficult to analyse and to respond to treatment.

As the Pope said during his 1982 visit to Liverpool:

> Unemployment is one of the major problems facing society as a whole. It sows seeds of bitterness, division and even violence. The young, unable to find a job, feel cheated of their dreams, while those who have lost their jobs feel rejected and useless. This tragedy affects every aspect of life, from the material and physical to the mental and spiritual. It therefore very much concerns the church.[11]

Trade unionists, and particularly Christian trade unionists, should not underestimate the human problems involved.

The initiative of the Lucas shop-stewards has been an indication of a trade unionism which reaches beyond traditional confines. In the mid 1970s Lucas aerospace jobs were in danger, so the workers, in what became known as 'The Lucas Workers' Alternative Plan', spelt out in detail a series of ways in which the combined sources of firm and operatives could be used for social needs production. Manufacturing of vehicles for disabled children was only one of many needs identified. The immediate plan failed to get the across-the-board backing required, but the idea has lingered on and similar ventures have been built on the original idea. Helen Wainwright, a leading exponent of the philosophy in her description of the project has rightly described what is going on as 'A New Trade Unionism in the Making'. This 'doing it for the community' approach to factory work is the germ of a powerful new idea which should be encouraged, particularly in areas of essential production where private enterprise has manifestly failed to respond.

The Lucas project has suffered from a dogmatic application of the 'financially viable' test – a doubtful test in many of the most important areas of human activity. Hopefully such trade union Pathfinders will be able to lift our assessment sights, as we search for alternative work patterns and activities.

Institutional Pathfinder

Surprisingly the government, albeit unconsciously, has been encouraging new work ethic alternatives which invite a reassessment of the measure of profitability. In a host of industrial training centres production is taking place which under the 'normal' economic system would not exist.

I cite as an example one of the 'new type' industries visited recently in a northern town. Over a hundred 'unemployed' young people were working in a converted textile factory. Engineering skills were being taught as renovation and repairs were carried out on vehicles owned by voluntary service groups from the district – i.e. a work experience no different from that offered in the private sector. The joinery and painting shops worked on equipment for handicapped children and prepared 'floats' for the future Lord Mayor's Show. A Third World tool centre collected gifts of equipment from well-wishers and 'dressed' the tools for distribution by Christian Aid or Oxfam; while a busy laundry shop met the needs of the Salvation Army and the Simon Trust. Other teams of youngsters were doing electrical and construction work on an adult education centre and a group of girls were acquiring sewing skills on costumes and decor for the local Arts Theatre. The entire labour force was fed in the 'factory' canteen by trainee cooks, while the administrative back-up was supplied as part of a secretarial course.

Money to pay for the project was provided by the government and the voluntary agencies; and all concerned benefited from the outcome.

But this was no 'factory' – it was a 'training centre'. 'Wages' were known as 'training grants' and 'jobs' were designated as 'courses'. No one was encouraged to call what was happening 'real jobs'. But the distinction becomes increasingly unreal once we are prepared to challenge the traditional work-wage relationship.

A new system is emerging – the 'contract' may not have been signed, but a deal is being done.

Many employers and unions prefer to think of such establishments as temporary or abnormal; but recognized or not, the activities constitute a revision of the work-wage relationship. In time, fuller acceptance of what is now 'new' will come, and proper accommodation within the social system will be provided for those who participate. The youngsters and those who support them are the first of the few, but the process will continue because it is attuned to the times. Future generations will wonder why we regarded the innovation as anything but natural.

But on closer inspection this 'new style' factory is not really very revolutionary. It is merely the extension to a new area of life of a principle which until now has had limited application: the principle that though today money profit is the dynamic for most of our economic activity, there will always be areas of human endeavour where financial gain cannot be the sole or main determinant. Already some of our most precious activities are famous 'loss makers', yet few would suggest their termination. How, for instance, do we measure the cost in upkeep of the 2294 sightseeing attractions listed by the English Tourist Board (1981) against the pleasure given to 157 million visitors?

Equally, a development like the Barbican Centre could hardly be justified as a 'money spinner'. Costing £153 million to build and £7 million a year to run, it must surely be financially another 'lame duck'. But it is part of a greater national arts complex with a turnover of £900 million and directly employing at least 200,000 people. It takes more than a calculating machine to measure the value of such as this – the profit to the nation is real but it is in terms of dignity and other intangibles.

Some of the most eagerly supported ventures have, in fact, little to do with the making of money. The *Mary Rose* enterprise of 1982 was a case in point – the fulfilment of a twenty-year old dream, to raise a 400-year old muddy hulk from the sea-bed. Its reappearance in October 1982, rescued with all the aids of modern technology in a £4 million operation, and attended by royalty and an enthusiastic media, might have seemed to those who confuse price and value as nothing more than a piece of black, smelly woodwork. But to the director of the project it was 'a fascinating and rare Tudor artefact'. The resurrection provided many months of work to hundreds of workers and happy excitement to millions of wellwishers. It was good work.

Such 'lame ducks' may be costly to maintain, but who would be without them?

For those who work on *Mary Rose* or at the Barbican the convergence of wage-job and creative employment is a considerable personal bonus – and in a real sense many of them would 'do the work for nothing'. When we learn how to extend the principle of such 'choice work' into other areas of activity, the new 'mix' called for between leisure and labour will be greatly facilitated.

Personal Pathfinders

Many of the challenges to conventional ways of earning a living have come in the development of basic communities of men and women who have come together to pioneer fresh life-styles and provide workable answers to such problems as the isolated family unit, the affluent society wasting and polluting the earth's resources, centres of learning where the medium stultifies the message, patronizing forms of social care and ineffective political involvement. David Clark's *Basic Communities* lists hundreds of such projects 'vigorously alive and filled with a hopeful enthusiasm and an optimism of grace which many of us gave up long ago'.[12]

The list is varied: some, world-famous names like Taizé, whose first stage culminated in 1974 when 40,000 young adults gathered to pray and plan action together for a better world, or the Corrymeela (Hill of Harmony) Ecumenical Community in Northern Ireland, whose practical work for peace is one of outstanding witness. Other groups are less well known, but equally dedicated; a Society of St John the Evangelist 'Anchorhold' Centre at Haywards Heath, which from 1969 has been developing prayer, meditation, and physical movement as part of a search for a richer Anglican spirituality; or the Othona Community, set up in 1946 to strengthen international relations, to foster Christian unity, to encourage a deeper experience of Christian community and to study the relations of faith and life with a view to action.

By no means all such communities are religious in membership, but the Christian influence is strong. New groups continue to be formed. The latest to announce a beginning came in 1982 from battered Northern Ireland. There, in an Irish Interchurch proposal, the Columbanus Community of Reconciliation is being organized to establish a residential community of Roman Catholics and Protestants 'committed to prayer and work for unity in the church, justice in society and peace on earth'. Sponsors came from the Church of Ireland, Methodists, Presbyterians, with a Jesuit and the Prior of a local CSSR monastery representing the Roman Catholics.

The name Columbanus is in memory of the sixth century Irish missionary who, in his zeal that the world might believe, set sail from his Bangor, Co. Down, monastery and established religious communities in Luxeuil (France) and Bobbio (Italy). Today's Ulster descendants of Columbanus believe that he, belonging to the period of the undivided church, challenges and encourages Protestants and Catholics to become reconciled to one another. They believe, too, that Columbanus is among those who, in the words of a recent inter-church report, have 'high expectations that initiatives will be boldly undertaken to deepen our reconciliation and lead us forward in the quest for the full communion to which we have been committed, in obedience to God, from the beginning of our dialogue'.[13]

It requires something of the faith of a Columbanus to set forth on such a venture in Northern Ireland these days; but the decision to found a new community at such a time is proof of the powerful call which the alternative communities idea generates.

Many of the most creative alternatives to a wage-dominated society have been more personal, offered in the life-styles of gifted or sometimes financially favoured individuals. Those, for example, with unearned wealth have long demonstrated their ability to 'get by' without wage work. By so doing they have often used their freedom to enrich their lives and that of society by personal spending on private work or by extending patronage to others. Many of our greatest estates and historic homes have been so maintained and the works of science and the arts have gained much from private endowments.

Others with a talent for earning money quickly have used the release available to give time for the works which they have regarded of greatest value. Sir Maxwell Joseph, who died a multimillionaire, boasted that he never worked more than a four-day week, leaving time for his charitable and personal interests. Richard Ingram of *Private Eye* runs that empire on a week-about basis; and Jimmy Savile's great work for charity is made more possible by having a very successful, but less than full-time, broadcasting career. Indeed, there is plenty of evidence from 'top people' that 'job-work' and 'real work' do not necessarily correspond and that the latter is of higher personal value.

Perhaps the doyen of them all is Bamber Gascoigne, who has done so much to enliven our viewing and our literature. In a recent *Daily Telegraph* profile[14] we learn that the happy accident of *University Challenge*, which is still going strong after 20 years, means that he is in effect paid a living wage for 40 days work a year. This active man, far from being stricken by the burden of 325 days 'unemployment', has been able to produce *The Christians* and other fine books. He has also turned a private passion for prints into a highly successful cottage industry.

There are a growing number of 'Bamber Gascoignes' in our midst doing 'a bit of this and a bit of that'. They are in the forefront of a new generation of life-style innovators who are finding time for the free play of creative energies beyond the confines of a wage-work relationship. One day, when we learn to value more equally what each according to their ability contributes to society, what is now a special privilege will be more generally enjoyed.

The black economy – is it all 'black'?

One other informal economic system which involves a new personal work 'mix', has been dubbed the 'black economy'. We can never be sure of how extensive the practice of having a job 'on the side' really is, but the Chairman of Inland Revenue estimates that it is 'not implausible' that Britain's black economy (i.e. income earned but not declared for tax purposes) might be as high as 7.5% of our gross domestic product. Estimates vary as to the numbers involved who work while receiving unemployment benefit, but a recent government report suggests that one in every twelve successful claimants for security benefit – or over 200,000 – got them by frauds. A report by Sir Derek Rayner, based on a sample survey of social security offices, put the figure for claimants in receipt of benefits, while they were in fact working, at 8%. In the worst cases, some of the officers believed that as many as 30% of successful claimants had a part-time job.

For that particular part of the black economy which we are considering – the unemployed – the haphazard structure of social security regulations has resulted in a chaos of anomalies which has lost it the respect of those who have to use the system – so the feeling that 'it is coming off a broad board' is widespread. In many ways the social security system encourages indolence and disrespect for the law and is a disincentive to do an honest day's work if a day's work is occasionally available – and for many of the benefit recipients, occasional work is all they are ever likely to be offered.

The term 'black economy' has become an umbrella term which is too broadly based – for example, those who use the system essentially for tax evasion purposes constitute a special problem, damaging to the economy. But as far as the unemployed and similar categories are concerned, there needs to be a 'whitening' of the market so that they may seek part-time work from which they can expect a reasonable return. The question certainly arises: if it is acceptable for those with high incomes to improve their incomes by taking on additional and sometimes highly-paid commissions, why must those at the bottom of the social ladder be discouraged from accepting a share in the informal economy by part-time work? We should encourage part-time work within a framework of regulations which encourage responsible citizenship.

As far as such casual manual labour is concerned, the black economy has grown and is likely to grow because of changing social patterns to do with home ownership, car repairs and many other acquisitions involving maintenance. It is particularly odd that society should frown on 'moonlighting' while at the same time deploring the 'neither work nor want layabout'. In fact the practice suggests that people are anxious to work. What needs to be examined is how far that part of the black economy represented by the unemployed who do an occasional job can be fitted into a social service scheme geared to current employment realities. Present insurance regulations assume a society where employment is full-time and where unemployment or part-time work is a passing phase.

The game has changed and so should the rules. Questions such as these would fit well into the agenda of a Standing Advisory Commission on Post-Industrial Society.

An educational expansion

So far we have been considering proposals which go somewhat beyond the traditional pattern of work, but during the transitional period there will also be need to identify areas of undone work which require community attention. Quite apart from work on an international scale which will test the zeal of many generations yet to come, there is a vast amount of work inside Britain which awaits attention. The environmental and inner city developments on which we have reflected earlier are cases in point, as are waiting lists for hospitals and other areas of social caring.

But by far the greatest single opportunity comes in education. It is a national cause par excellence – one on which it would be reasonable to expect a consensus. Our failure to cope with this issue is a measure of our inability to grasp the opportunities of the present, and the needs of the future. Indeed, more than any other sector of social development education is what the future of our nation is all about. Some calculations for the year AD 2000 foresee a labour force requirement in the educational/information sector as high as 50%.

It is also in our economic interest to spend more on education: as

Germany and Japan have illustrated, there is a vital link between educational standards and industrial advance. But the signs are not good. Thousands of teachers are unemployed while children throughout the nation flounder in overfull classes, and further education facilities are being reduced as the student applications rise. At times Wells seems to be right: we are losing the race between education and catastrophe.

The contradictions (representing missed opportunities) are obvious and alarming. There is, for instance, a suggestion in discussions about the teaching profession that we have a surplus of teachers in the United Kingdom. Such statements make strange reading when they appear alongside statistics of nationwide overcrowding. A recent plan by the National Union of Teachers gives evidence of the seriousness of the situation. In what is regarded as a considerable improvement the Union calls for 60,000 extra teachers for the 30,000 schools within the state system. Added to the present teaching force of 460,000 this would make possible groups of 23 in infant reception classes, 20 in nursery classes and 27 in primary and secondary schools. Such classes are anything but small, given the standards required for (and deserved by) our children.

The proposal is hardly likely to find official acceptance, but by any standard it is a modest one. The number of classes (often in the most deprived areas) of over 30 has been described by the NUT as a 'national scandal'. In one London Borough more than one-quarter of the classes have more than 35 children; even more favoured Oxfordshire averages 32 a class.

Some of the worst educational neglect takes place where unemployment is highest and where it might be expected that the school at least would provide an oasis which children could enjoy and in which they might obtain the educational back-up to compensate for the social deprivation of their community. Sadly, the reverse is true – if you live in a deprived area then more than likely your school will suffer too.

From reports received from teachers throughout the country I quote the contrasting experiences of one young teacher who, after working in a comprehensive in the north-east, moved to a well-known public school in the south. She stresses the importance of directing more resources into the state system:

During my term's teaching practice I learned a few home truths about the current situation in local comprehensives, to balance the rather overtly philosophical advice we were receiving in the University Lecture Theatre.

The concern to meet children's needs is valid enough, but the tendency to look for complicated psychological definitions for under-achievement and anti-social behaviour amongst young adults has, it seems to me, obscured more straightforward suggestions for improvement. I believe that injections of capital into many secondary schools could vastly improve educational and social standards.

Our school was structurally unsuitable for any serious study. It was built to hold 500 and now over a thousand children fill every inch of space. General space has had to be used for classrooms, and teaching groups often shared the same assembly hall. Locker space and even desks were in short supply. To make matters worse, the stock of books was pitifully low – no library book was let out of school.

I am not saying that money would solve everything, but it would give more essential space – space for movement and privacy, with smaller and more manageable groups. Lack of funds has starved and is strangling the school and the classes of well over 30 were unmanageable. The teachers try hard but they are fighting against impossible odds. However, with proper support, *and especially financial backing*, the staff could do wonders to restore confidence, results and attitudes among kids who really need help.

I am now teaching at a wealthy public school where the children are manifestly the same – bar the accent – as those at my comprehensive. What they have is not so much social advantage (many wealthy boarders have outrageously deprived backgrounds in emotional terms) but environmentally they have facilities at school to stretch their wings and experiment and grow up in space with style. Money could do this for the state sector. I find the urges within the state system to whip children away to special schools, to label them 'educationally subnormal' and 'imbalanced' through social disadvantage are elaborate though irrelevant alibis for much simpler – though less fashionable – problems.

Even allowing for a certain amount of post-College of Education impatience with educational theory, the contrast brought out in this short, sharp experience bears witness to the point that in education, as in other areas of social provision, the need for investment is both great and urgent. In the light of such examples it is hard to disagree with the NUT assessment of pupil teacher ratio as 'a national scandal'. It would be costly, but given a right balance of priorities in our national spending the bill could be met.

Education is not the only area in which much-needed job expansion might take place during the period of industrial readjustment which faces us: it is only the most obvious item of unfinished 'social business' to which we should attend, now that we are favoured with an available 'surplus' labour force. We forget, too, that unemployment is not free. It must be paid for and the cost (even in financial terms) is high. Estimates vary. Two years ago, Jenkins and Sherman estimated the cost to the government of an unemployed man with two children and an average mortgage as being over £3,200 a year.[15]

A more recent survey by the WEA suggests that the first year's bill to the state when a married person with two children and earning £6,000 loses his job may be as high as £6,207. The calculation:

	£
Income Tax	1,060
Indirect Tax	247
N.I. contribution	1,043
Unemployment benefit	2,258
Family Income Supplement	231
Rent & Rates Rebate	441
Free School Meals	156
Administration Cost	156
Redundancy Pay	615
	£6,207

(Source WEA Unemployment Pack 1982: Scope, Oct. 1982)

But beyond the monetary cost of unemployment there is a far greater *real* cost – a cost in terms of what is done to the fabric of society when large numbers feel 'shut out' of normal community involvement. The alienation is all the greater when it is manifestly a nonsense to argue that there is no work to be done.

In this respect what needs to be challenged again and again is the assumption that unemployment is necessarily related to the amount of work available. Hopefully the activities of our various Pathfinders will reveal this contradition and direct us to a truer measurement of the value of work and a shift away from notions which measure 'profitability' solely or primarily in terms of a financial calculation. Our existing political institutions do not encourage flexibility in thought or experimentation; too often they confine the debate within an unreal adversary framework.

We return to an earlier conclusion: forty years on from Sir William Beveridge's great Report on the Welfare State we are in need of a new social contract, geared to current national needs and able to draw on a significant amount of inter-party vision for its implementation. We also need for our day and generation something of the spirit of national unity which accompanied the post-war reconstruction.

In another place[16] I have argued a case for the 'sufficient society' – a society based on public policies which would encourage social unity; which will transcend 'left' and 'right' and ensure an equitable sharing, both at home and abroad, of our considerable wealth. The 'yardstick' of national morality offered by Richard Titmuss still stands:

> I submit, the fundamental test of the effectiveness and morality of different economic and social systems is not whether they are richer or not. What is fundamental is how we use and distribute our increasing affluence; the extent to which we deny ourselves to benefit others; and the degree to which we bring under public control the exercise of arbitrary economic powers.[17]

It has been a central theme of this book that we are not limited by our resources, but by the use to which we put those resources. The battle against poverty has been long and hard, but it has been won if we have the good sense to share the available gifts of sufficiency – in particular, to begin the process of turning spears into pruning hooks. As a modern prophet puts it: 'Till now, man has been up against Nature; from now on he will be up against his own nature.'[18] These are truths that can make us free.

At a more immediate level (and for many what matters most) we face the fact that the 'right to work' (wage need) can no longer be guaranteed within the framework of the market economy – people are now being ejected from the factory system to which they went in a previous age when they were divorced from the land. There can be no 'Poor Law', so we must move in the direction of a right to subsistence for those who cannot find outlets for their talents. The 'social wage' required would need to be at a level to make possible for the recipient a meaningful membership of society; it also follows that there will be a blurring of the distinction between what we have traditionally known as wages and income.

What is clearly indicated is the creation of a 'double' or 'dual' economy; 'market' and 'service'. Informally, the system is already with us in embryo – the idea now requires acceptance by national planning agencies as the centrepiece of economic strategy, and not as a temporary response to changes in market conditions. Again, the recognition that we face the end of an era is paramount.

The 'market' sector (mainly manufacturing) would be capital intensive and highly effective in terms of productivity, concentrating on the creation of the home and foreign material trading requirements of the nation. It would be the wealth base on which the community would survive materially and maintain its place in the industrial and commercial league. The partner economy would be the 'service' sector, with its emphasis on national social needs; labour intensive, it would major in the growing demands of educational, welfare, environmental and leisure activities. Together, the dual sectors would encourage a new flexibility and offer 'choices' which correspond to natural talent. 'Work' and 'activity' would begin to merge; in the cross-fertilization, life would be transformed.

The 'dual economy', though relatively simple to outline, would require a social and moral 'mix' of a high order: ready adaptation on the part of organized labour and management and, above all, a national willingness to permit and encourage an economic order in which the co-operative ethic would dominate the competitive urge.

It is a price that can be paid, must be paid, and is well worth paying for social justice and communal stability. It will not be easy to make the shift in emphasis, but increasingly the alternatives to social co-operation is community confrontation. The social 'sums' involved require a good deal of thought, but the thinking has started. The Professor of Employment at Manchester University has gone so far as to put a figure on the new divide:

> Those outside the market divide (it may be well to plan for 20% of the labour force at any one time) must be enabled, on the basis of guaranteed subsistence, to contribute to the social and environmental quality of our society. Both types of work need to be done; both confer human dignity on the doer. It will not be easy

> to devise arrangements whereby a working life-span will consist of 80% worked in the market economy and 20% in the social environmental sector. But the sooner a start is made, the sooner the scourge of unemployment will be lifted.[19]

Britain is well placed to pioneer a 'New Model' – a society which will take us beyond the arid confrontations of dogmatic Capitalism and doctrinaire Marxism. Industrial experience, the capacity to adjust to social change and the strength of democratic traditions give the nation a creative potential.

Already the potential is being proclaimed as significant changes in attitude *do* take place: the cross-bench movements in politics, new partnerships in industry, the twinning of a Brandt and a Heath, growing support for increasingly radical public 'training' schemes. Above all, we can draw encouragement from the examples of self-help schemes by people in community from every region who, by taking their destinies into their own hands, are creating an alternative, and more fulfilling, society.

The maps for the future are being made – the mapmakers must be encouraged. Hopefully, too, a qualitative change may come into our thinking as many begin to sense that we need measurements of what is good in society which go beyond mere price. Value is also being weighed. Even our economic advisors make the point:

> I am more and more convinced that the problem is not at heart a technical problem capable of a technical solution, but a moral problem concerned with the values of our age. We cannot consider the growth of technology or the growth of government as autonomous forces which are somehow independent of the set of values which have either accompanied or promoted their growth. Obedience to Christ demands change – selfishness is transformed to love.[20]

Selfishness tranformed to love – there's the rub.

Such affirmations are timely: they warn and encourage as we confront the shadow and substance of work. In particular, we are reminded from the market-places of life that earthly disciplines deal only with the 'simple arithmetic' of our existence; we begin to discover the 'higher calculus' which is essential for all who consider the human condition.

APPENDIX

Church Action with the Unemployed: Job Creation Guide

(*reproduced by permission*)

Create new jobs

What unemployed people most want is a job. Starting a new business is one of the solutions. Could your church join with others to start a new business in your area, using existing local resources and skills?

Small businesses are now big business! They employ one third of the nation's workforce and produce one fifth of the national income. Starting up in business is not necessarily easy, but, despite the recession, it was recently reported that 2,500 new small firms open every week.

In areas where traditional industries are facing decline and extinction, unemployed people are starting up new firms on their own, or together with others in the community. They have faith in their skills and abilities, use their redundancy money as start-up capital and get extra finance from the banks or from the European Economic Community. They also get help from their former employers. They use the opportunity to run their own lives for a change.

A practical way of expressing Christian love and concern is to help set up a new small business providing goods and services, and jobs, for people. This leaflet tells you how to get started.

Small firms service

The Government has appreciated the importance of the small firm sector. It has recently introduced a wide range of measures to help.

The Department of Industry has launched its 'Business Opportunities Programme' backed up by a 'Small Firms Service'. Nationwide there are 11 small firms centres and 50 area counselling offices. They provide information and advice on all aspects of setting up and managing a new firm. They have excellent pamphlets and leaflets to help.

Which type of organization?

You may want to start a new business, either on your own or together with others, along conventional lines. But consider the possibility of doing something different. Consider starting a co-operative enterprise. They have a special role to play in creating new jobs.

Forming a co-operative is a convenient way for a small group to constitute itself as a corporate legal entity, with limited liability. It is a form of self-help and it offers the real satisfaction that can come from working for yourself, and for one another.

There has been a significant increase in the number of co-operatives registered recently. They offer a new form of working relationship and can have various characteristics. Here are two types:

A. Neighbourhood co-operatives

The Co-operative Development Agency (CDA) has worked with the National Council for Voluntary Organizations (NCVO) to develop a model for organizing neighbourhood co-operatives. They aim to meet local needs, such as small repair work, child care, energy conservation or small-scale retailing. They help people who recognise the potential, have the skills and are looking for work, but are not sure how to take advantage of the opportunities.

A neighbourhood co-operative is owned and controlled by its members, who may be small in number and who can, under its legal rules, fall into three categories. It can have:

1. Full-time members, who work full time and derive their main income from the co-operative through a weekly wage;
2. Part-time members, who are paid an hourly rate, though without any upper or lower limit on the number of hours worked;
3. Volunteers, who take on occasional work and are unpaid, though they may receive an annual sum in recognition of their contribution.

B. Common ownership companies

Common ownership companies have been defined by the Industrial Common Ownership Act 1976 and are also corporate bodies with a legal status. Unlike other co-operatives, only those employed by the enterprise have the right to be members, and this becomes mandatory after an initial qualifying period.

Shares are normally of £1 value and are restricted to one per member. They do not provide all the necessary capital. This has to be raised in the form of loan stock and re-invested profits. Control of the enterprise is always retained by the members, and they share responsibility for management, business practices and the allocation of profits. Frequently a proportion of the profits is used for charitable or social purposes, both inside and outside the company.

If a common ownership enterprise is closed down, its assets have to go to another similar organization, or to an agency promoting this type of company, or to a charity. This stops a company being dissolved for reasons of personal gain and ensures that what may be a viable means of local employment is protected.

Essential first steps

Whether you plan to start a conventional small business or a co-operative, get clear in your mind what the aims of your business are. Is there a real market for your product or service? Is your idea good enough to sustain the necessary investment?

Discuss your project (in strict confidence) with one of the Small Firms Service counsellors. They have business experience and the first session is free.

Finance

Work out preliminary costings, a profit and loss budget and a trial balance sheet.

Get help and advice from a bank manager. Ask about the Government Loan Guarantee scheme. It can guarantee the repayment of loans up to £75,000, repayable over two to seven years, and is specifically designed to provide capital for small businesses and co-operatives to invest in fixed assets.

If you are a part of a voluntary or community group running a neighbourhood co-operative, seek help from the Manpower Services Commission.

Find out about other help from the Government. It has introduced a wide range of tax incentives, reduced rates of corporation tax, increased depreciation allowances for capital expenditure, tax relief on losses and on interest paid on borrowings.

Premises

Ask about Government agencies and local authorities which provide new small factory units for rent or purchase, and about special grants and rate exemptions available in Development Areas and Enterprise Zones.

Find out if there is a 'Local Enterprise Trust' or 'Business Promotion Centre' in your area, bringing together information about available premises, skills, resources, needs and finance.

In rural areas, sponsor a public meeting together with the Parish Council to look at employment needs. Local attitudes to planning applications can help or hinder the development of opportunities for work in villages. Help to shape positive attitudes on this.

Ask about money from the Social Fund or the Regional Development Fund of the European Economic Community.

And staff

Get advice from the Job Centre or Employment Office about people who might come and work with you and about skills available in your area. Ask them to advertise your vacancies.

Ask about subsidized training schemes for adults or young people available through an Industrial Training Board or the Manpower Services Commission.

Useful addresses and contacts

National Agencies

Action Resource Centre, 9 Henrietta Place, London W1M 9AG.
Co-operative Development Agency,
20 Albert Embankment, London SE1 7TJ.
Council for Small Industries in Rural Areas,
141 Castle Street, Salisbury, Wiltshire SP1 3TP.
Department of Industry, Small Firms Division,
123 Victoria Street, London SW1E 6RB.
Industrial Common Ownership Limited,
The Corn Exchange, Leeds LS1 7BP.
Job Ownership Limited, 42 Hanway Street, London W1P 9DE.
Manpower Services Commission (Special Programmes),
Selkirk House, 166 High Holborn, London WC1V 6PF.
National Council for Voluntary Organizations,
26 Bedford Square, London WC1B 3HU.
National Youth Bureau, 17/23 Albion Street, Leicester LE1 6GD.
Youthaid, Tress House, Stamford Street, London SE1 9NT.

Local Organizations

Careers Service
Chamber of Commerce or Trade
Citizens' Advice Bureau
Council of Churches
Diocesan Board for Social Responsibility
Industrial Mission Team
Job Centre or Employment Office
Technical College
Trades Council
Trade Union Branches

Other leaflets in this series:
Coping with Unemployment, Training and Work Experience Schemes, Creating New Jobs, Church Action with the Unemployed. Available free from: Church Action with the Unemployed, Campaign Office, PO Box 576, Aston, Birmingham B6 5QL.

The 'Church Action with the Unemployed' Campaign is promoted by a group of people from the major Christian churches in Britain who are concerned about unemployment and social responsibility, chaired by Canon Frank Scuffham, industrial chaplain in Corby. It has been paid for by grants from the central funds of the supporting churches and from charitable trusts, with additional help from the Manpower Services Commission.

NOTES

1. The Withering of Work

1. Ernest Bevin, *My Plan for 2,000,000 Workers*, Clarion Press 1933, pp. 5–6.
2. *The Observer*, 3 January 1983.
3. *The Times*, 3 November 1982.
4. E. F. Schumacher, *Good Work*, Jonathan Cape 1979, p. 61.
5. *The Guardian Weekly*, 7 November 1982.
6. Martin Mayer, *Today and Tomorrow in America*, Harper & Row 1976, p. 69.
7. Foreword to Brian Showler and Adrian Sinfield, *The Workless State*, Martin Robertson 1981, p. xiv.
8. See *New Internationalist*, No. 112, June 1983, special edition on Ageing.
9. Giles Merritt, *World Out of Work*, Collins 1982.
10. Claude Geffre, *International Review of Mission*, WCC, October 1982, p. 486.

2. A New Covenant with the Machine

1. Robert Tressall, *The Ragged Trousered Philantropists*, Penguin 1944, p. 62.
2. See *The Economist*, 4 December 1982.
3. *House of Lords Journal*, February 1812.
4. *Daily Telegraph*, 2 November 1982.
5. 'Automation and the Office Worker', APEX 1980, pp. 3, 4.
6. See *Scientific American*, special edition on The Mechanization of Work, September 1982.
7. J. M. Keynes, 'Economic Possibilities for our Grandchildren', 1930, reprinted in *Essays in Persuasion*, Macmillan 1933.

8. Hannah Arendt, *The Human Condition*, University of Chicago Press 1958, pp. 4, 5.
9. Norbert Wiener, *The Human Use of Human Beings*, NY 1950, pp. 97f. Quoted by Dennis Gabor in *Inventing the Future*, Penguin 1963, p. 97.
10. Address to British Institute of Management, November 1979.
11. John Davy Interview, *The Observer*, 15 August 1982.
12. Giles Merritt, *World Out of Work*, Collins 1982, p. 63.
13. David Bleakley, *In Place of Work . . . The Sufficient Society*, SCM Press 1981, p. 68.
14. Gabor, op. cit., p. 110.
15. Hazel Henderson, *Creating Alternatives Futures*, Berkley Publishing Corporation 1978, p. 401.
16. Ibid., p. 402.
17. *Scientific American*, September 1982, p. 155.

3. Compulsory and Compulsive Work

1. Bertrand Russell, *In Praise of Idleness*, Allen & Unwin 1958, p. 26.
2. Clive Jenkins and Barrie Sherman, *The Leisure Shock*, Eyre Methuen 1981, p. 2.
3. Russell, op. cit., p. 23.
4. F. S. Fiorenza, *Work and Religion*, T. & T. Clark 1980, p. 97.
5. For an excellent summary, see J. A. C. Brown, *The Social Psychology of Industry*, Penguin 1954, p. 202.
6. Edmund Burke, 'A Vindication of Natural Society', *The Works of Edmund Burke, Vol. 1*, World Classics 1906, p. 47.
7. George Orwell, *Selected Writings*, Heinemann 1963, p. 34.
8. John Burnett, *Useful Toil*, Allen Lane 1974, p. 14.
9. Ibid., p. 226.
10. *The Times*, 15 November 1982.
11. *The Observer*, 19 December 1982.
12. Herbert Marcuse, *Eros and Civilization*, Sphere Books 1972, p. 17.
13. Bertrand and Dora Russell, *The Prospects of Industrial Civilization*, Allen & Unwin 1959, p. 278.

4. Profile of those in Special Need: UB40 People

1. Fred Kemp et al, *Coping with Redundancy*, Hamlyn Paperbacks 1981, p. 11 and introduction.
2. Recommendation 948 (1982), Records of Parliamentary Assembly of the Council of Europe.
3. House of Lords Official Report, Vol. 436, No. 6, 16 November 1982.
4. Dennis Marsden, *Workless*, Croom Helm 1982, p. 2.

5. David Sheppard, *Bias to the Poor*, Hodder & Stoughton 1983, p. 19.
6. *Despite the Welfare State*, DHSS 1982, p. 304.
7. Ibid., p. vii.
8. Ibid., p. 64.
9. Elaine Brown, *Grounded*, Lion 1982, p. 92.
10. *BMA Journal*, col 1630, 19 December 1981.
11. *BMA Journal*, col 1180, 11 April 1981.
12. Based on materials researched by A. Edgar Stevens FRCS, Hindhead, Surrey.
13. Colin Bedford, *Weep for the City*, Lion 1982, p. 9.
14. Adrian Sinfield, *What Unemployment Means*, Martin Robertson 1981, p. 187.

5. A Role for the Church

1. *United Kingdom Christian Handbook*, Bible Society 1983, p. 2.
2. William Temple, *Christianity and the Social Order*, Penguin 1956, p. 24.
3. Ibid., p. 51.
4. Ibid., p. 74.
5. Ibid., p. 74.
6. Ibid., p. 29.
7. William Neil, *Bible Commentary*, Hodder & Stoughton 1973, p. 247.
8. David F. Wright, *Essays in Evangelical Social Ethics*, Paternoster Press 1978, p. 9.
9. See Introductory Essay by David F. Wright, *Essays in Evangelical Social Ethics*, p. 7.
10. John Stott in *Essays in Evangelical Social Ethics*, p. 181.
11. David Sheppard, *Bias to the Poor*, Hodder & Stoughton 1983, p. 218.
12. *The Guardian*, 8 September 1981.
13. See Nicholas Deakin, 'Why Nothing Seems to Work in the Inner Cities', *The Guardian*, 7 September 1981.
14. Martin Conway, Audenshaw Paper No. 83, January 1982.
15. See Claude Geffre, 'Theological Reflection on a New Age of Mission', *International Review of Mission*, WCC, No. 284, October 1982.
16. Sheppard, op. cit., p. 225.

6. A Practical Response to the Work Crisis

1. See Campaign Leaflet, *The Time for Action is Now*, Birmingham 1982.

7. *Transcending the Work Ethic*

1. Lewis Mumford, *The Condition of Man*, Secker & Warburg 1944, p. 5.
2. Kenneth Clarke, *Ruskin Today*, Penguin 1982, p. 270.
3. Mumford, op. cit., p. 4.
4. Harvey Cox, *The Secular City*, SCM Press 1965; Penguin 1969, p. 192.
5. See Clifford Longley, 'Treating Unemployment as a Sin', *The Times*, 30 August 1982.
6. For a contemporary discussion on these points see Silvano Burgalassi, 'Towards a Theology of Man as a Worker', *Concilium*, Vol. 131, 1980.
7. R. A. Markus, 'Work & Worker in Early Christianity', in J. M. Todd, *Work*, Darton, Longman & Todd 1960, p. 13.
8. E. F. Schumacher, *Good Work*, Jonathan Cape 1979, p. 2.
9. Patrick McGrath in John M. Todd, *Work*, p. 43.
10. Jean Remy, 'Work and Self Awareness', *Concilium*, Vol. 131, 1980, p. 5.
11. Quoted by Kenneth Clarke, *Ruskin Today*, Penguin 1982, p. 264.
12. Leading Article, *Manchester Examiner & Times*, 2 October 1860.
13. From 'Pre-Raphaelitism'. Quoted by Clarke, op. cit., p. 280.
14. Ibid., p. 264.
15. Quoted in Ivor Clemitson and George Rodgers, *A Life to Live*, Junction Books 1981, p. 6.
16. Clemitson and Rodgers, op. cit., p. 22.
17. Ibid., p. x.
18. H. G. Wells, *Men Like Gods*, Victor Gollancz 1933, p. 1062.
19. See David Bleakley, *In Place of Work . . . The Sufficient Society*, SCM Press 1981, p. 44.

8. *Pathfinders: Coping with the Great Transition*

1. H. G. Wells, reprinted in *The Observer Review*, 28 December 1980.
2. Richard Fothergill in the *Schoolmaster and Career Teacher*, July 1982.
3. John Davy, 'The Man in the Belly of the Beast', *The Observer*, 15 August 1982.
4. Quoted by Harvey Cox, *The Secular City*, Penguin 1969, p. 194.
5. Roger Clarke, *Work in Crisis*, St Andrew Press 1983, p. 209.
6. David Brown, *All Their Splendour*, Collins Fount 1982, p. 221.
7. *The Times*, 29 June 1982.
8. Quoted in Hazel Henderson, *Creating Alternative Futures*, Berkley Publishing Corporation 1978, p. 72.
9. *New Internationalist*, June 1982, p. 10.
10. John A. Murdock, 'Changing Attitudes Among Ageing Americans', *Contact*, WCC, November 1981.
11. *The Times*, July 1982.

12. David Clark, *Basic Communities*, SPCK 1977.
13. For Information on the Society: Columbanus Community, c/o Corrymeela, Ballycastle, Co. Antrim.
14. *Daily Telegraph*, 12 July 1982.
15. Clive Jenkins and Barrie Sherman, *The Leisure Shock*, Eyre Methuen 1981, p. 51.
16. David Bleakley, *In Place of Work . . . The Sufficient Society*, SCM Press 1981, Chapter 7.
17. R. M. Titmuss, *Essays on the Welfare State*, Allen & Unwin 1963, pp. 215f.
18. Dennis Gabor, Inventing the Future, Penguin 1963, p. 89.
19. *The Times*, 2 September 1982.
20. Brian Griffiths, *Morality and the Market Place*, Hodder & Stoughton 1982, p. 154.

INDEX